Patriotic Crafts

I HEAR AMERICA SINGING, THE VARIED
CAROLS I HEAR.

WALT WHITMAN

Patriotic Crafts

60 Spirited Projects that Celebrate America

Chris Rankin

LARK BOOKS

A Division of Sterling Publishing Co., Inc.
New York

Editor: Dawn Cusick
Art Director: Megan Kirby
Photographer: Evan Bracken, Light Reflections
Cover Designer: Barbara Zaretsky
Production Assistance: Shannon Yokeley
Editorial Assistance: Delores Gosnell

Library of Congress has cataloged the earlier edition as follows:
Rankin, Chris.
    Patriotic crafts : 60 spirited projects that celebrate America / Chris Rankin.
    p. cm.
    Includes index.
    ISBN 1-57990-428-9
    1. Handicraft. 2. Patriotism in art. 3. Americana in art. 4. Americana in interior
    decoration. I. Title.

    TT157 .R34 2002
    745.5—dc21

2002030105

10 9 8 7 6 5 4 3 2 1

Published by Lark Books, a division of
Sterling Publishing Co., Inc.
387 Park Avenue South, New York, N.Y. 10016

© 2002, Lark Books

Distributed in Canada by Sterling Publishing,
c/o Canadian Manda Group, 165 Dufferin Street
Toronto, Ontario, Canada M6K 3H6

Distributed in the U.K. by Guild of Master Craftsman Publications Ltd.,
Castle Place, 166 High Street, Lewes, East Sussex, England BN7 1XU
Tel: (+ 44) 1273 477374, Fax: (+ 44) 1273 478606,
Email: pubs@thegmcgroup.com, Web: www.gmcpublications.com

Distributed in Australia by Capricorn Link (Australia) Pty Ltd.,
P.O. Box 704, Windsor, NSW 2756 Australia

If you have questions or comments about this book, please contact:
Lark Books, 67 Broadway, Asheville, NC 28801, (828) 253-0467

Manufactured in China

ISBN 1-57990-428-9 (hardcover) 1-57990-793-8 (PLC)

For information about custom editions, special sales, premium and corporate purchases, please
contact Sterling Special Sales Department at 800-805-5489 or specialsales@sterlingpub.com.

TABLE OF CONTENTS

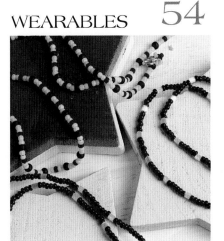
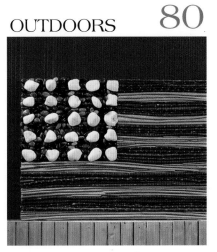

INTRODUCTION

The color combination of red, white, and blue evokes a barrage of feelings and memories for most of us. During happy times, they are the colors of patriotic holidays, 4th-of-July fireworks, and summer barbecues. At other times, they are the colors of our flag, waved in recognition of incredible sacrifices by individuals and families. At still other times, they are the colors of our country, symbols of a spirit and optimism that unities us as a nation.

After a recent national tragedy, our country seemed to become draped in red, white, and blue. Stars and stripes became in vogue design elements, showing up as motifs on everything from new dishware lines to car magnets. Even our country's symbol of hard-fought freedom, the flag, became a marketing icon, decorating

WORDS LIKE "FREE-DOM" "JUSTICE," "DEMOCRACY" ARE NOT COMMON CONCEPTS; ON THE CONTRARY, THEY ARE RARE. PEOPLE ARE NOT BORN KNOWING WHAT THESE ARE. IT TAKES ENORMOUS AND, ABOVE ALL, INDIVIDUAL EFFORT TO ARRIVE AT THE RESPECT FOR OTHER PEOPLE THAT THESE WORDS IMPLY.

JAMES BALDWIN

t-shirts, delivery trucks, college basketball team jerseys, pizza boxes, and even the logos of the major television networks.

Patriotic design elements are far from new, though. Crafters and artists and crafters have explored Americana themes for centuries through folk art. Many antique quilts, woodcarvings, weather vanes, rugs, and embroideries are graced with patriotic designs, and their patriotic imagery is as strong and meaningful today as it was years ago.

This book offers a variety of craft projects designed to celebrate the colors and symbolism of red, white, and blue. Some, such as the window box, banner, and lantern, let you share your patriotic spirit with the world. Other projects are more personal expressions, decorating

THERE IS BUT ONE UNCONDITIONAL COMMANDMENT, WHICH IS THAT WE SHOULD SEEK INCESSANTLY, WITH FEAR AND TREMBLING, SO TO VOTE AND TO ACT AS TO BRING ABOUT THE VERY LARGEST TOTAL UNIVERSE OF GOOD WHICH WE CAN SEE

WILLIAM JAMES

the body or the home with projects such as jewelry, scarves, candles, and pillows.

Public patriotism, with its bright banners and waving flags, may serve a national need, but many of us also have a much more personal need: a need to create with and display patriotic colors as artists and crafts people, to express our love of country in the things we make.

NEARLY ALL MEN CAN STAND ADVERSITY, BUT IF YOU WANT TO TEST A MAN'S CHARACTER, GIVE HIM POWER.

ABRAHAM LINCOLN

HOME DECORATING

Although red, white, and blue may not be in the color palette of your current home decor, their design versatility is truly amazing.

They can be used in primary colors with a bright white, or they can be toned down with white-washed hues and ivory. For more formal look, mix them with brass, copper, silver, or gold.

The projects in this chapter offer a variety of design ideas. You can create something practical (the Waving Stripes Sand Candles on page 12) or something whimsical. Create focal point for a room (the Mountain Star Flower Wall Quilt on page 40) or a subtle accent for a corner (the Patriot's Potpourri on page 34). Make a gift for your favorite someone (Handmade Cards, page 12) or a cherished keepsake (the Decoupaged Journal on page 26).

WAVING STRIPES SAND CANDLES

These candles can be made in minutes, so you can easily use them to decorate every place setting for your next special occasion and send them home with guests as party favors. The wavy layers are created when you press the candle in place. For variation, add layers of blue sand, or fill the votives with a single color of sand.

WHAT YOU NEED
Clear glass votive containers
Red craft sand
White craft sand
Small spoon
White votive candles

1 Cover the bottom of a votive container with a thin layer of red craft sand. Gently shake the container to flatten the sand.

2 Use a spoon to shake an even layer of white craft sand over the red layer.

3 Continue adding layers of sand in alternating colors until you have filled about two-thirds of the container with sand.

4 To create the waves, gently press the votive candle into the center of the sand until the top of the candle rests just below the container's rim. If you have too much sand or don't like the effect, just empty the container and start over.

I BELIEVE THAT EVERY RIGHT IMPLIES A RESPONSIBILITY; EVERY OPPORTUNITY, AN OBLIGATION; EVERY POSSESSION, A DUTY.
JOHN D. ROCKEFELLER, JR.

DESIGNER: MEGAN KIRBY

HANDMADE CARDS

Handmade gestures of patriotic spirit are perfect for sending Fourth of July, Presidents' Day, Veterans' Day, and Memorial Day salutations. The cards were made with antique toy flags and antique Christmas tinsel, although flag scrapbooking paper and pipe cleaners can be substituted.

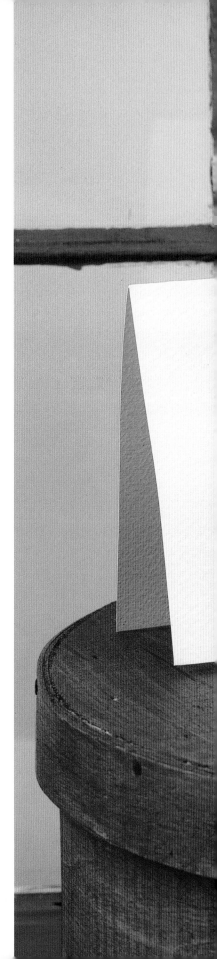

WHAT YOU NEED
Toy flags
Blank stationery cards
White craft glue
Large-eyed needle and metallic thread
Antique Christmas tinsel
Star sequins, optional

1 Cut the toy flags into strips and glue them to the card. Finger press to remove any air bubbles and allow to dry completely.

2 Press holes around the perimeter of the flag with the tip of the needle, spacing them about every ½ to 1 inch. Bend the tinsel (or pipe cleaner) around the flag.

3 Working with a threaded needle on the back side of the card, come up through the holes you made in Step 2, go over the tinsel, and then go back down through the same hole. Continue attaching the tinsel in this way until you have worked your way around the flag. Tie off and trim thread.

Variation: Add sparkle by gluing star sequins to the card.

GOD BLESS AMERICA, LAND THAT I LOVE.
IRVING BERLIN

MISTS OF AMERICA PHOTO FRAME

Create a patriotic montage of stars and stripes with this colorful photo frame. Since the effects of overspraying are somewhat unpredictable, you'll be constantly surprised by the effects produced by these masking and color blending techniques.

WHAT YOU NEED

Floral design spray paints in white, blue, and red

Wood frame

Precut plastic stripe stencil

2 precut plastic star stencils, one large and one small

Masking tape

Clear, high-gloss spray varnish

1 Set up a work space in a well-ventilated area, preferably outdoors. Cover your work area with newspaper or a drop cloth, then spray paint the wood frame with a thin, even coat of white paint, taking care to cover all of the frame's visible edges. Allow the paint to dry completely, then add additional coats if needed until you achieve a smooth saturation of color. Let dry.

2 Position a stripe stencil at an interesting angle across the painted frame and secure in place with a small piece of rolled masking tape. Lightly spray red paint across the stencil, sweeping past its edges. Allow the paint to dry completely, then gently remove the stencil. Repeat this process in several locations with different colors of spray paint.

3 Tape a star stencil to the frame. (Feel free to adhere this stencil over previously painted areas.) Lightly spray the paint across the star stencil, sweeping past its edges. Allow the paint to dry completely, then gently remove the stencil. Repeat this process in several locations using both star stencils and all colors of spray paint.

4 Repeat Steps 2 and 3 to fully decorate the frame.

5 Following the manufacturer's instructions, spray the wood frame with a thin, even coat of clear, high-gloss spray varnish, taking care to cover all of the frame's visible edges. Allow to dry completely before handling.

Designer Tip: White spray paint can be very useful in fine-tuning your design. If you feel that any area is sprayed too dark or looks muddy, just tape down a new stencil and spray over it with white paint. The white can also provide a new background for further stencilling.

DESIGNER: MARTHE LE VAN

NAPKIN RINGS

Add a patriotic touch to any place setting with these red, white, and blue beaded napkin rings. They can also be used to add a splash of color around the house — on bedposts, doorknobs, etc.

WHAT YOU NEED

For each napkin ring

3 brass star beads, with a hole going through the center

1 yard elastic beading thread, 0.5mm

Blue seed beads, size 8/0

Red seed beads, size 6/0

3 rectangular white beads, 14mm long

1 Thread a brass star bead onto the middle of the elastic beading thread, then thread two blue, a red, three more blue, and a red seed bead onto each side of the star.

2 Pass both ends of the thread through a rectangular bead so they come out on opposite sides.

3 Thread one red, three blue, a red, and two blue seed beads onto each side of the rectangular bead.

4 Add a star bead, passing both ends of the thread through it.

5 Repeat steps 2 through 4 until you have strung the last rectangular white bead.

7 Repeat the pattern from Step 3, then pass both ends of the thread through the first star bead you put on to close the napkin ring.

8 Tie a knot around the thread coming out of the star bead with each free end of the thread. Pass the thread back through the star bead and cut the excess thread away.

THE SHALLOW CONSIDER LIBERTY A RELEASE FROM ALL LAW, FROM EVERY CONSTRAINT. THE WISE MAN SEES IN IT, ON THE CONTRARY, THE POTENT LAW OF LAWS.

WALT WHITMAN

DESIGNER: CHRIS RANKIN

AFTERNOON DECK GLASSES

The faux airbrush technique used on these glasses is created with overlapping layers of stencils and paint. The technique creates subtle variations in colors and patterns, making each glass a celebrated individual.

WHAT YOU NEED

- 12 heavyweight glasses
- Mild detergent
- Rubbing alcohol or surface conditioner made for prepping glass (available at craft stores)
- Cotton swabs or clean cloth
- Masking tape
- Star stickers of various sizes made for scrapbooking (available at craft stores)
- Old newspapers
- Spray glass paint in red, white, and blue
- General-use spray acrylic finish (optional)
- Tweezers (optional)
- Mineral spirits (optional)

1 Wash the glasses thoroughly with warm soap and water, and dry well to remove all dirt.

2 Apply a coat of rubbing alcohol or surface conditioner with cotton swabs or a clean cloth. Allow the surfaces to dry completely.

3 Use small strips of overlapped masking tape to mask off the bottom rim of each of the glasses. (Note: Small strips round curves more easily.)

4 Use the same masking technique to cover the rims and the top sections of each glass, leaving at least enough room to prevent a user's mouth from touching painted areas. Cover the opening of each glass with horizonal layers of tape.

5 Arrange the scrapbook stickers in a random design of your choice on the unmasked surfaces of the glasses, then place the glasses upright in a row on a newspaper-lined surface outdoors.

6 Shake each of the paints thoroughly before using, following the manufacturer's directions. Spray a bit of paint on a scrap of newspaper to get a feel for how quickly you will need to move your hand to create the desired effect. Avoid pausing as you spray to prevent streaking and globbing.

7 Beginning with the white paint, apply a light coat of color over the sides of the glasses. Turn the glasses slightly, then add another light coat of a different color. Continue adding light layers of paint to create an airbrushed effect.

8 Allow the paint to dry completely, referring to the manufacturer's directions, then add a light coat of acrylic finish to seal the paint. Allow the glasses to dry completely.

9 Carefully remove the stickers, using a pair of tweezers to grab the edges if needed, and remove the masking tape.

10 Remove any paint that has seeped beneath the tape with mineral spirits or turpentine. Wash the glasses well before use.

PATRIOTIC SEAL CANDLES

These candles haven't won any medals, but they look like they're wearing them! As the candles burn down, just remove the ribbon and wax seal and recycle them. A similar effect can be created with polymer clay if you prefer.

WHAT YOU NEED
Wax paper
Patriotic seal and
   sealing wax
Small metal spoon
Wire-edged ribbon
Candles
Glue gun

1 Spread a sheet of wax paper on a flat work surface. Prepare your wax seal by placing it on top of an ice cube. (A chilled seal sets hot wax quickly and is less likely to stick.)

2 Place a small piece of sealing wax in the metal spoon. Hold the bottom of the spoon over a lit votive candle until the sealing wax becomes a liquid. If the wax begins to smoke or sputter, hold the spoon a little farther away from the flame.

3 Pour the wax onto the waxed paper in circles just a little larger than your seal. Quickly press the seal into the wax. You will probably need to experiment with the amount of wax needed to make a nicely shaped sealing wax medallion. If you aren't happy with your results, just remelt the wax and try again.

4 Measure and cut a length of ribbon to fit around the candle. Twist each end of the ribbon and secure if necessary with a glue gun. Hot-glue one end of the ribbon to the center front of the candle, then wrap the ribbon around the candle and hot-glue the opposite end in place.

5 Gently peel the wax paper away from the medallions, then hot-glue a medallion to the candle where the ribbon ends meet.

THE WAY TO BE PATRIOTIC IN AMERICA IS NOT ONLY TO LOVE AMERICA, BUT TO LOVE THE DUTY THAT LIES NEAREST TO OUR HAND, AND TO KNOW THAT IN PERFORMING IT WE ARE SERVING OUR COUNTRY.
WOODROW WILSON

DESIGNER: MEGAN KIRBY

AMERICA-THE-BEAUTIFUL BATH SOAPS

Use the translucence of glycerin to your artistic advantage by arranging stars, flags, or other decorative ornaments in between the layers of these colorful soaps. Your favorite fragrance can also be added.

WHAT YOU NEED
Several bars of uncolored glycerin soap
Small saucepan or double boiler
Thermometer
Soap molds
Red and blue food coloring
Butter knife

1 Cut the soap bars into thirds. Place a third of the soap into the saucepan or double boiler. Melt slowly at low heat. (Heating at temperatures over 160° F may cause your finished soaps to sweat.)

2 When the soap has completely melted, add several drops of red food coloring. Blend in the food coloring, stirring gently to avoid creating foam.

3 Place the molds on a flat surface. Slowly pour the melted soap into the molds until they are one-third full, then remove any surface bubbles with the butter knife. Allow the glycerin to harden completely (about 1 hour).

4 Clean the pan well, then repeat the melting, pouring, and hardening process to add a middle layer of clear glycerin and a top layer of blue glycerin.

5 Allow the soap to harden for several hours before removing from the mold. Store unused soap in plastic wrap in a dry place.

ONE MAN WITH COURAGE MAKES A MAJORITY.
ANDREW JACKSON

DESIGNER: MEGAN KIRBY

DESIGNER: MEGAN KIRBY

DECOUPAGED JOURNAL AND BOOKMARK

This colorful journal and bookmark were created with antique postage stamps. The journal would be perfect as a travel diary to record memories of your United States travels. The stamps were found in an antique shop, and a large package of them was just a few dollars.

JOURNAL

WHAT YOU NEED
Sheet of decorative paper
Journal
Rubber cement
Assortment of stamps
Decoupage medium
Small paint brush
Blue ribbon or binding tape

1 Cut a square from the decorative paper about ⅛ inch smaller than the inside cover of the journal.

2 Lay the journal on a sheet of newspaper. Cover the front of the journal with a coat of liquid rubber cement. Arrange the stamps on the journal front, overlapping them in a pleasing pattern and allowing them to hang over the edges of the journal by ½ inch on the top, bottom, and right-hand sides.

3 Apply a coat of liquid rubber cement on the inside of the journal cover. Fold the stamps over the edges of the journal. Measure and cut a piece of decorative paper to fit the space and press in place.

4 Brush a coat of decoupage medium over the stamps and allow to dry completely.

5 Cut a piece of blue ribbon or binding tape that's twice the length of the height of the journal plus ½ inch. Position the center of the ribbon on the left side of the journal and glue it in place to cover the raw edges of the stamps. Smooth the ribbon in place to remove any bubbles or folds, then fold the ribbon around and glue it in place on the inside of the journal, overlapping the ends as needed.

BOOKMARK

1 Cut out a rectangle from the cardboard using the pattern on page 112. Place the cardboard on a piece of protective newspaper and apply a coat of liquid rubber cement to the top surface.

2 Arrange your favorite stamps on the cardboard piece, overlapping them in a pleasing pattern. (The rubber cement will allow you to rearrange the stamps if you wish.) Allow the rubber cement to dry completely.

3 Turn the cardboard face down and cover the back with a coat of rubber cement. Press a piece of decorative paper over the rubber cement, smoothing out any air bubbles or wrinkles. Trim off any excess paper.

4 Punch a hole about ⅛ inch from the center top of the bookmark. Brush on a coat of decoupage medium and allow to dry completely, then thread a tassel through the hole.

STARBRIGHT BOXES

These easy-to-make boxes are perfect for patriotic keepsakes or for special gift boxes. For a different effect, consider lining the boxes with fabric or patterned paper.

WHAT YOU NEED
Star-shaped cardboard boxes
Red, blue, and gold acrylic paint
Paintbrush
Red and blue rhinestones
Glue gun
Gold glitter glue

1 Paint the inside of the star boxes in blue or red and allow to dry completely.

2 Paint the outside of the boxes and lids gold and allow to dry completely.

3 Hot-glue a rhinestone to the center of each box top, then outline the rhinestone with glitter glue.

DESIGNER: MEGAN KIRBY

ETCHED OIL LAMPS

These flames burn brightly for several hours (and no dripping wax), making them perfect for parties and other gatherings.

WHAT YOU NEED

Glass oil containers with flat edges

Red, blue and clear lamp oil

Etch cream

Craft knife

Self-adhesive vinyl with peel-off backing

Small squeegee

Straight-edged ruler

Star and stripes stencils (or paper to make your own from templates on page 112)

Carbon paper

Pick out knife (optional)

Cotton swabs

STRIPES

1 Wash and dry glass. Etch the two back sides of each lamp first. (If one side has a seam from the mold, use it as the back side.)

2 With scissors or craft knife, cut eight ½-inch-wide strips of vinyl, making sure that at least one long edge of each strip has a good

H OUSTON, TRANQUILLITY BASE HERE. THE EAGLE HAS LANDED.

NEIL ARMSTRONG

DESIGNER: DIANA LIGHT

clean cut line. Arrange the strips in a border around all sides of the two back panels. To ensure good contact between the vinyl and the glass, create your border line about $\frac{1}{16}$ inch in from the edges of the lamp.

3 Fingerpress the vinyl strips in the areas where they overlap to prevent the etching cream from seeping under the gaps and causing uneven patterns.

4 Doublecheck the vinyl for good adhesion, then clean off any adhesive residue that may be left on the glass with a cotton swab moistened with water.

5 Cut eight 2-inch-wide strips of vinyl, four of them a little longer than the bottle's width and height. Add these on to strip borders to widen the borders so that no cream will spill onto areas you don't want etched.

6 Nestle lamps in towels rolled and bunched to keep lamps from rolling.

7 Review the manufacturer's instructions well, taking care to stir well and use adequate ventilation.

8 Use one hand to support the wide strip on one side and carefully pour etch cream on to vinyl strip. Then, using squeegee, quickly and evenly pull cream over exposed glass.

9 Wait for time as designated by the manufacturer, then rinse cream off and remove vinyl under water. Allow to completely dry before handling.

THE TRUTH IS FOUND WHEN MEN ARE FREE TO PURSUE IT.
FRANKLIN DELANO ROOSEVELT

STARS

There are two version of star lamps shown here: one with the stars etched, the other with the background etched and the stars showing in the background.

For the etched background with the clear stars:

1 Lay the border like the back panels. Add wide border strips also.

2 Carbon copy the star pattern onto the vinyl. With scissors or craft knife, cut out stars, taking care not to overcut or cut into the stars at all.

3 Peel off the vinyl stars and finger press the remaining vinyl tightly against the glass, checking for good adhesion. Remove any excess adhesive with a cotton swab dampened with water.

4 Use one hand to support the vinyl and carefully pour etch cream on to vinyl strip. Then, using squeegee, quickly and evenly pull cream over exposed glass.

5 Wait for time as designated on bottle. Then rinse cream off and remove vinyl under water. Allow to completely dry.

For the etched star version:

1 Carbon copy the star stencil to the vinyl, leaving a 2-inch border around the stencil. Position and stick stencil to panel to be etched.

2 With craft knife, cut out stars, taking care not to overcut into the stencil background. Pull stars out carefully with a craft knife. Place peel-off backing over stencil and squeegee over it to ensure good adhesion.

I WOULD RATHER BE EXPOSED TO THE INCONVENIENCES ATTENDING TOO MUCH LIBERTY THAN THOSE ATTENDING TOO SMALL A DEGREE OF IT.
THOMAS JEFFERSON

3 Remove any excess adhesive with a cotton swab dampened with water.

4 Use one hand to support the vinyl and carefully pour etch cream on to vinyl strip. Then, using squeegee, quickly and evenly pull cream over exposed glass.

PATRIOT'S POTPOURRI

Patriot gardens have become popular again, and they're a great source for red, white, and blue dried flowers. (Your local craft store is another great source!) To prevent the colors from fading, avoid displaying the potpourri in a sunny location.

WHAT YOU NEED
Assortment of dried flowers and seed heads in red, white, and blue
Brown paper bag
Essential oil in fragrance of your choice

1 Place your dried materials in the bottom of a brown paper bag and add 2-3 drops of essential oil.

2 Remove any excess air from the bag and roll it up tightly, then shake gently. Place the potpourri in a decorative bowl and enjoy.

Tip: Essential oils will lose their potency over time. Repeat the process to refresh the scent when needed.

Good Choices for Red Blooms
Rosebuds
Globe amaranth
Strawflowers
Zinnias
Tulips

Good Choices for White, Silver, or Ivory Blooms
Lamb's ears
Pussy willow
Sage
Silver king artemisia
Dusty miller
Globe thistle

Good Choices for Blue Blooms
Globe thistle
Blue salvia

THESE ARE TIMES IN WHICH A GENIUS WOULD WISH TO LIVE. IT IS NOT IN THE STILL CALM OF LIFE, OR IN THE REPOSE OF A PACIFIC STATION, THAT GREAT CHALLENGES ARE FORMED... GREAT NECESSITIES CALL OUT GREAT VIRTUES.

ABIGAIL ADAMS

DESIGNER: MEGAN KIRBY

STAR PILLOWS

Decorative pillows are easy to make and can be custom-embellished to suit your home's decor. Gold ribbon, vintage military buttons, and whimsical fringe are just a few of the many options.

WHAT YOU NEED

¼ yard burgundy plush felt

¼ yard blue plush felt

8- x 24-inch piece of ivory plush felt

Polyester fiberfill

2½ yards braided upholstery trim

2 1-inch (2.4 cm) buttons

Fabric glue

1 Enlarge the pattern on page 113 to the size indicated. For each pillow, cut four pieces from the burgundy felt, four from the blue felt, and two from the ivory felt.

2 Select two of the cut pieces in different colors and place their right sides together. Pin the upper seams of the shapes together between the star and dot symbols on the pattern. Machine-stitch the pieces together with a ⅜-inch seam at the pinned area.

3 Repeat Step 2 to join the remaining pieces, alternating the colors as you work.

4 Repeat Steps 2 and 3 to make a second pieced star.

5 Pin the two pieced stars together with their right sides facing. Stitch together with a ⅜-inch seam allowance, leaving a 4-inch opening for turning.

6 Trim the seam allowance at the points of the star, and clip to the stitching line at the seams. Turn right sides out. Press fiberfill into the star points with scissor tips, then stuff the remainder of the pillow. Slipstitch the opening closed.

7 Attach trim around the edges of the pillow at the seam with fabric glue. Finish by stitching a button to the center front of both sides of the pillow.

THE WAVE OF THE FUTURE IS NOT THE CONQUEST OF THE WORLD BY A SINGLE DOGMATIC CREED BUT THE LIBERATION OF THE DIVERSE ENERGIES OF FREE NATIONS AND FREE MEN.
JOHN F. KENNEDY

DESIGNER: BARBARA MATTHIESEN

RED, WHITE, & BLUE BEESWAX TAPERS

These naturally scented beeswax candles burn with a subtle aroma reminiscent of honey. Beeswax sheets can be found in a myriad of colors in most craft stores, and these candles take just minutes to make.

WHAT YOU NEED

One sheet each of red, white, and blue beeswax

Hair dryer

Small kitchen knife

Metal ruler

Wick #500 (burns longer) or #360 (burns brighter)

1 Gently warm the sheets of beeswax to room temperature with a hair dryer. They should be pliable, not brittle.

2 Working on a flat surface, cut a 3- x 8-inch rectangle from each of the three sheets of beeswax with the knife. Use the edge of the ruler to ensure a straight edge.

3 Stack the sheets on a flat surface and align their edges. The bottom sheet will be the outside layer of the candle.

4 Cut a piece of wick about 1 inch longer than the length of your candle. Lay the wick ¼ inch from the edge of the stacked sheets. Gently fold the wax over the wick, then press down to secure the wick firmly in place.

5 Roll the candle as tightly as you can, taking care not to damage the honeycomb pattern and leaving 1 to 1½ inches of the beeswax unrolled. Trim the edges of the stacked beeswax even, then finish rolling the candle. Gently squeeze the bottom of the candle into a shape that will fit your candleholder.

I T IS TIME TO PROVIDE
A SMASHING ANSWER
FOR THOSE CYNICAL
MEN WHO SAY THAT A
DEMOCRACY CANNOT BE
HONEST, CANNOT BE
EFFICIENT....
WE HAVE IN THE DARKEST
MOMENTS OF OUR
NATIONAL TRIALS
RETAINED OUR FAITH IN
OUR OWN ABILITY TO
MASTER OUR OWN
DESTINY.

FRANKLIN D. ROOSEVELT

DESIGNER: MEGAN KIRBY

MOUNTAIN STAR FLOWER WALL QUILT

This patriotic wall quilt can be cut and pieced in a weekend, and portions of the design can be used to create matching couch pillows or table runners. The white areas create the perfect place to showcase your favorite quilting patterns, or you can use a simple all-over quilting design.

WHAT YOU NEED

⅔ yard cotton navy #1
¾ yard navy #2
1½ yards navy #3
⅔ yard red #1
1 yard red #2
3 yards white cotton fabric
50-inch square piece of batting
Thread to match

1 Sew template C pieces to template A pieces, then press to navy side. Sew one of the above pieces to each of template C pieces. Sew these pieces together to form the square in Figure 1.

2 Continue sewing all other pieces together to form 16 squares. Sew each of these squares

CUTTING INSTRUCTIONS; TEMPLATES ON PAGE 116

*From navy #1, cut 64 pieces from template A.
*From navy #2, cut 4 crosswise strips 2¾ inches wide and 40 pieces from template D.
*From navy #3, cut 4 strips lengthwise of the fabric 2½ inches wide.
*From red #1, cut 64 pieces from template B and four 2½-inch squares.
*From red #2, cut 4 crosswise strips 2¾ inches wide, 5 crosswise strips 2½ inches wide, and 24 pieces from template D.
*From the white, cut one rectangle measuring 43 x 50 inches and one 10 x 50 inches. Cut 4 strips measuring 11½ x 30 inches (extra length has been included) and 4 strips measuring 2 x 48 inches (you are given extra length). Cut 64 pieces from template C.

GENERAL NOTES

You have been given extra length on the strips to allow for the differences in machines, so adjust these lengths to the side of your given quilt if necessary. Use ¼-inch seams throughout and be careful not to stretch the bias sides while sewing.

DESIGNER: JUANITA METCALF

together to form the larger square in the center of the quilt. Refer to the photo as needed.

3 To form a white border around the center squares, sew two 1½ x 30 strips to opposite sides of the square. Trim and press, then repeat with remaining two sides.

4 Piece four triangles as shown in Figure 2. Add the strip borders, making sure you leave enough extra fabric to cut a 45-degree angle on the ends of the strips. Sew these triangles to opposite sides of the center square. (The side of the triangle is bias, so be sure you do not stretch as you sew to the square.) Add the 2½-inch borders from navy #3 with the squares of red #1 added in the corners.

5 Cut the selvages from the white. Sew the 43- x 50-inch rectangle to the 10- x 50-inch rectangle to form the backing of the wall quilt. Press.

6 Layer the backing, batting, and quilt top. Secure together and quilt as you like. You may hand or machine quilt; this quilt was machine quilted.

7 For binding, take the five 2½-inch strips from red #2 and cut the ends on a 45-degree angle. Sew

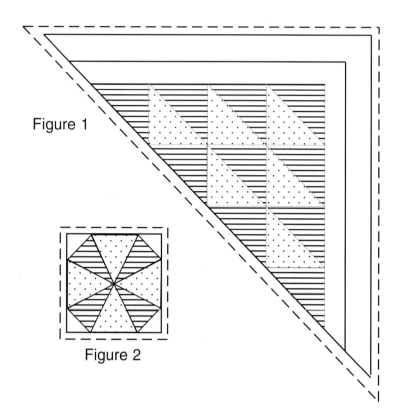

Figure 1

Figure 2

the strips together to form one continuous long strip. Press seams. Fold the strip in half lengthwise and press.

8 Sew the binding strip to the right side of the quilt, mitering the corners. Fold the binding to the back and handstitch in place. Add a 4-inch sleeve on one end for hanging.

THE BOISTEROUS SEA OF LIBERTY IS NEVER WITHOUT A WAVE.
THOMAS JEFFERSON

STRIPED
LAMP SHADE

Here's a simple way to dress up a plain lamp shade for special holidays and occasions.

WHAT YOU NEED
White or ivory lampshade
Red and white acrylic craft paint
1-inch-wide sponge brush
Measuring tape and glue gun
Blue ribbon trim

---

1 Paint the lampshade red. After the paint has dried, place the shade over the lamp and turn on; if you see streaks, add a second coat.

2 With a measuring tape and pencil, make even marks at the top and bottom of the lamp shade to guide in painting the stripes. Using a sponge brush, paint red stripes from top to bottom and allow to completely dry.

3 Measure lengths of ribbon for the top and bottom of the shade by wrapping ribbon around the shade. Add an inch to the lengths and cut.

4 Add a ring of glue around the top edge of the shade and press the ribbon into the glue. As you near the starting point, fold the edge of the trim back ¼ to ½ inch (trim excess ribbon if needed), and glue over the bottom ribbon. Repeat with the bottom edge of the shade.

DESIGNER: MEGAN KIRBY

FESTIVE HOLIDAY ORNAMENTS

Most craft stores sell a variety of three-dimensional, easy-to-paint glass ornaments. The paints used in these ornaments easily cover painting imperfections, so give yourself permission to play.

WHAT YOU NEED

Glass tree ornaments

Glass surface conditioner (refer to your paints for specific manufacturer recommendations)

Air-dry opaque glass paints in red, white, blue, gold, and brown

Stencil and craft knife

Small round brush

Flat brush

Fine detail brush

Cotton swabs

GENERAL INSTRUCTIONS

1 Clean and dry glass, handling carefully to prevent breakage. Apply a coat of surface conditioner with the flat brush, referring to the manufacturer's instructions.

2 Cut stencils for the desired patterns using the patterns on pages 114 and 115.

3 Paint the ornaments, referring to the photos for colors and patterns and to the information below for specific tips. Use the round brush for borders, stripes, and covering large areas, and the detail brush for finer work. Be sure to rinse your brushes well and pat them dry between colors.

DESIGNER NOTES

To make dots, dip the handle of the brush in red paint and then lightly touch it to the glass.

For ornaments with stripes: If your stripe edges are too uneven, moisten a cotton swab with surface conditioner and use it to even up the lines while the paint is still wet.

For the bell ornament, mix gold and brown paints together for the main surface. Paint the stripe across the top and the crack in brown; use gold for the lettering and the bell clapper, then highlight the crack with a thin gold line.

THE BASIS OF OUR POLITICAL SYSTEM IS THE RIGHT OF THE PEOPLE TO MAKE AND TO ALTER THEIR CONSTITUIONS OF GOVERNMENT
GEORGE WASHINGTON

DESIGNER: DIANA LIGHT

BEAD-EMBELLISHED CANDLE

Add a burst of patriotic color and texture to a plain candle with a few simple materials. Memory wire, a popular material with many jewelry makers, is easy to maneuver, holds its shape well, and is a great way to showcase your favorite beads.

WHAT YOU NEED
6 coils of bracelet memory wire
Round-nosed pliers
Red and blue India glass beads, 10 mm long
White seed beads, size 6/0
Wire cutters
White pillar candle, slightly thicker than the coils of memory wire

1 Make a loop in one end of the memory wire with the round-nosed pliers.

2 String a red, white, blue, and another white bead onto the wire. Repeat this pattern until you reach the other end of the memory wire.

3 Make a loop in the other end of the memory wire as you did in Step 1.

4 Trim any excess wire with the wire cutters.

5 Wrap the memory wire around the candle, securing if needed with a dab of hot glue.

FREEDOM IS AN INDIVISIBLE WORD. IF WE WANT TO ENJOY IT, AND FIGHT FOR IT, WE MUST BE PREPARED TO EXTEND IT TO EVERYONE, WHETHER THEY ARE RICH OR POOR, WHETHER THEY ARE WITH US ON NOT, NO MATTER WHAT THEIR RACE OR THE COLOR OF THEIR SKIN.

WENDELL LEWIS WILLKIE

46

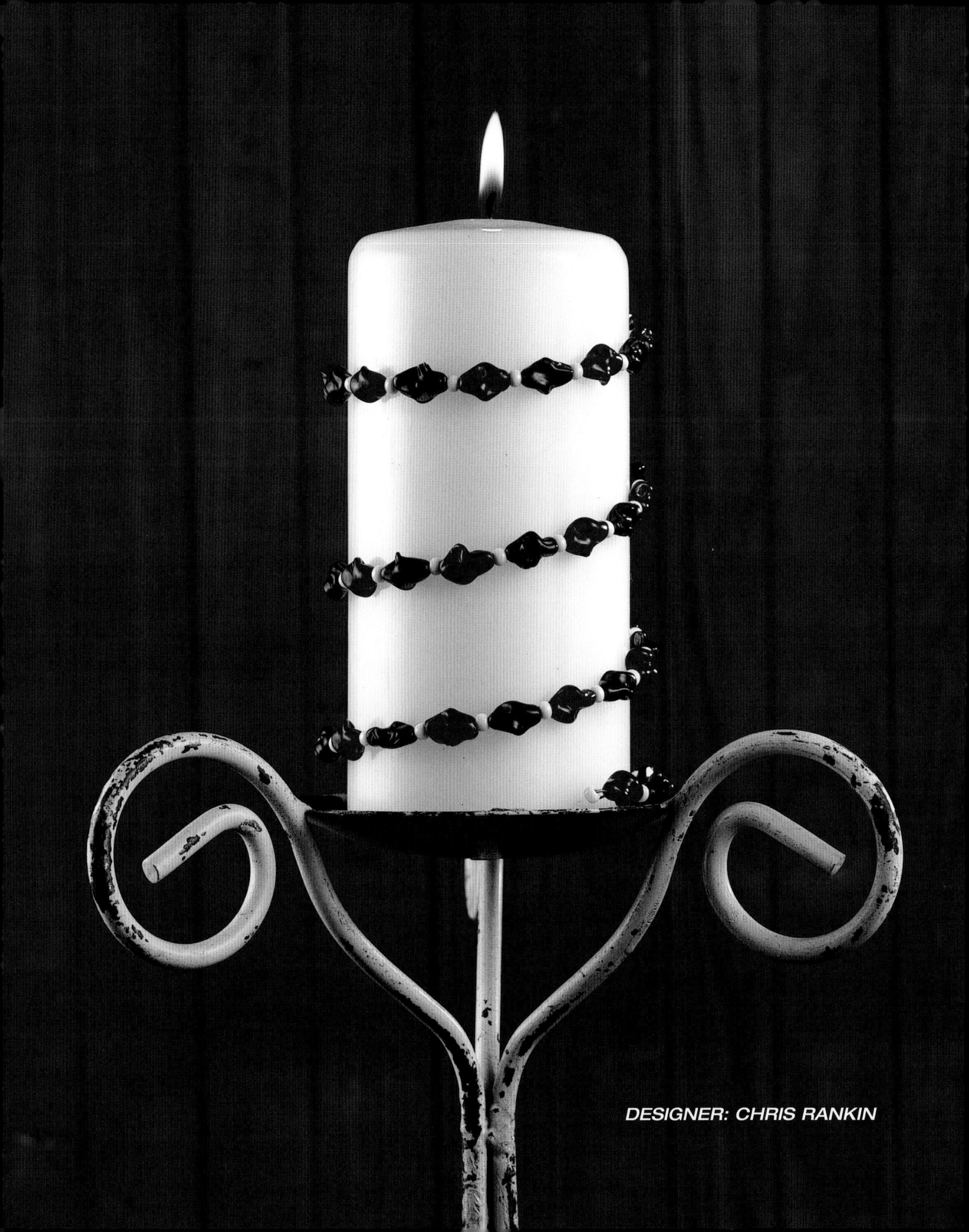

DESIGNER: CHRIS RANKIN

DESIGNERS:
CATHERINE HAM
AND SALLY POOLE

PATRIOTIC AFGHAN

Thirty-five crocheted blocks were assembled to create this striking afghan. The number of blocks can very easily be adjusted to make an afghan of any size, from a baby blanket to a lap robe to a king-sized bedspread.

ABBREVIATIONS

chain = ch

chains = chs

slip stitch = slip st

single crochet = sc

double crochet = dc

half double crochet = hdc

WHAT YOU NEED

9 balls navy, 2 balls white, and 2 balls red in Plymouth Yarn Company's Encore worsted weight yarn (75% acrylic, 25% wool)

Hook size US H/8 (metric 5 mm) or size needed to achieve gauge

Flag applique, optional

GAUGE

Rows 1-10 should make a rectangle measuring approximately 9 X 6 inches.

FINISHED SIZE

Approximately 50 x 54 inches as shown here, but size can be varied to suit personal preferences.

TO MAKE ONE BLOCK

The navy portion of the block is crocheted in ribbed or ridge double crochet; this is worked as double crochet except that the hook is inserted into the back top loop instead of into both loops.

Measure 60 inches into the navy yarn. Make a slip knot at the 60-inch mark and loosely ch 32 from the ball side of the navy yarn.

Row 1: Dc into 3rd ch from hook inserting the hook into back loop of ch, and in each ch, for a total of 30 dc.

Row 2: Ch 3, turn, dc into each dc, inserting hook through the back loop only. (30 dc)*

Rows 3-10: Repeat row 2.

The top and right side of the block should be facing you now. Mark the block by tying a small piece of contrasting thread to a stitch to make it easier to keep all blocks in the same direction when joining. Using navy yarn and right side facing, turn work and continue on the short side as directed in Rows 11-14.

Row 11: Insert hook into top of last dc, ch 1, sc into dc leg, sc into dc of last dc of row 9. Continue along the short side to the starting ch, sc. Finish off.

Row 12: Working with the 60-inch length of navy yarn, insert hook into ch, ch1, continue as for Row 11 on the second short side. Finish off.

Rows 11 and 12 should give a smooth finish to make a neat edge for the color change. Make sure the block lies flat and is not pulled too tight.

Change to white yarn.

Row 13: This row is worked in the round. With right side facing, join white yarn at any place, ch 2, hdc into all loops from previous row. Working 3 hdc into each corner loop, slip st into first hdc. Finish off.

Change to red yarn.

Row 14: With right side facing, join red at any place, ch 1, sc into all loops of previous round, working 3 sc into each corner loop, slip st into first sc. Finish off.

Make a total of 35 blocks for the size shown here or alter the number of blocks if a different size is desired.

FINISHING

Double-check to make sure that all blocks are the same size. Arrange the finished blocks 5 x 7 so that all face in the same direction and slip stitch or crochet them together.

To form the edging, working with red yarn and right side facing, join the yarn with a slip stitch in the back loop of any sc, ch 1, and continue in ribbed sc around the afghan, working 3 sc in each corner, until you have worked back to the first sc. Slip stitch into the first sc and fasten off. Darn in any loose ends. Sew the flag applique, if desired, neatly in a corner.

IF WE CANNOT NOW END OUR DIFFERENCES, AT LEAST WE CAN HELP MAKE THE WORLD SAFE FOR DIVERSITY.
JOHN F. KENNEDY

50

SHOOTING STAR CANDLE

Decorate your plain, ordinary candles with shooting stars reminiscent of Fourth of July fireworks. Gold glitter glue was used for these candles, but other colors can be used for special effects.

WHAT YOU NEED
7 gold star buttons with sew-on backs
Flat-sided blue pillar candle
Glue gun
Screwdriver
Glitter glue

1 Press the star buttons into the front face of the candle. If necessary, use a screwdriver to scrape small indentations in the wax to accommodate the button backs. Secure the buttons in place with glue.

2 Create shooting star lines for each star with glitter glue, starting on the button and working outward. Allow to dry completely before moving.

DESIGNER: MEGAN KIRBY

STARS & STRIPES CLOCK

Take time out for this fun painting project. Advanced painting skills are not required, and the clock mechanism is simple to attach. For a more opaque effect, consider using flat paints instead of frosted paints.

WHAT YOU NEED

- 9-inch square of ¼-inch-thick glass with center hole
- 9-inch square piece of self-adhesive vinyl with peel-off backing
- Small squeegee
- Carbon paper
- Craft knife
- 2 pieces of cardboard
- Glass spray paints in frosted white, frosted blue, and frosted red
- Cotton swabs
- Mineral spirits
- Clock movement for ¼-inch-thick clock face

1 Clean and dry the glass. Unpeel the top half inch of the vinyl backing and press the vinyl against the glass. Press out any air bubbles with the squeegee, then continue unpeeling the vinyl and removing air bubbles. Save the vinyl's backing sheet for later.

2 Increase the patterns on page 118 as directed. Use carbon paper to transfer the numbers and stars to the vinyl, referring to the photo as a guide.

3 Outline the patterns with a craft knife, then peel away the background vinyl, leaving just the numbers and stars. Place vinyl backing over glass and press the squeegee over the glass to ensure good contact between the vinyl patterns and the glass. Remove any adhesive residue on the glass with a cotton swab moistened with water.

4 Prepare a well-ventilated work area (preferably outdoors) with several layers of newspaper. Place a piece of cardboard over two-thirds of the back side of the glass, leaving a 3-inch vertical strip on the left side.

5 Spray the exposed area with an even layer of blue paint, then slide the cardboard over about ¼

inch and spray this area very lightly to create a blending area between colors. Allow the paint to dry completely.

6 Place one piece of cardboard over the far right 3 inches and another over the newly painted blue section, leaving the middle 3 inches plus the blending area exposed. Spray this area with white paint. Move the right-hand piece of cardboard over ¼ inch and lightly spray with white paint to create a blending area between the white and red stripes. Allow paint to dry completely.

7 Cover the blue and white areas (except for the blending area) and spray with red paint. Allow to dry completely.

8 Carefully remove the numbers and stars from the glass, using a craft knife to lift off the edges if necessary. Remove any adhesive

DESIGNER: DIANA LIGHT

residue on the numbers and stars with cotton swabs moistened with water. Use a craft knife to chip away any dried paint mistakes or dab them away with a cotton swab moistened with mineral spirits.

9 Attach clock movement to center back of glass.

T RUE PATRIOTISM HATES INJUSTICE
IN ITS OWN LAND MORE THAN
ANYWHERE ELSE.

CLARENCE DARROW

WEARABLES

This chapter features a variety of projects to create unique, patriotic wearables. You'll find everything from subtle, understated nods to patriotism to colorful, look-at-me displays.

The scarf on page 60, for example, uses a deep blue velvet fabric embellished with stamped stars and a gold bead trim. The decorated T-shirt on page 68 greets the world with a graphic display of stars and stripes.

Many of the projects take just an hour or two (see the Star Spangled Earrings on page 67), while others, such as the Patriotic Sweater on page 64, take a little longer. You can add decorative touches to purchased items (see the Streaming Stars Beret on page 70) or make something completely from scratch (see the Patriotic Hat and Scarf on page 63).

TRI-COLOR SCARF

Create a spirited scarf in red, white, and blue. The same technique can also be used to make a lap blanket or afghan — just increase the width and number of rows.

Advanced level

Foundation: Chain 24 with white yarn.

Row 1: Dc in 3rd st from hook, dc across, turn (22 sts).

Row 2: Ch 3, sk the 1st dc and work 1 dc in next dc. * Ch 2, sk the next 2 dc, work 1 dc in each of next 2 dc. * Repeat across, working last dc in top of turning ch and add blue yarn with the last yarn over of the last st. Turn. Leave white yarn at the side of the work; carry it up the side of the work when it is needed again.

Row 3: Using blue yarn, ch 2, sk 2 dc, then work a dc in each of the next 2 sts skipped on the first row, encasing the ch 2 bar of the last row in ea dc as it is made. Continue to work ch 2 over the 2 dc of the last row and a dc in each of the skipped sts in the two rows below to the end of the row. Complete the row with ch 2, working a sl st in the top of the turning ch. Add red by drawing a loop of yarn through the sl st. Leave the blue at the side and carry it up the side when it is needed again. Turn.

Row 4: Ch 3, work a dc in the 2nd st two rows below, encasing the ch 2 worked in the last row. Continue working ch 2 over the 2 dc of the last row, and a dc in each of the skipped sts two rows below. Complete row by working a dc in the skipped st two rows below and a dc in turning ch (where blue yarn was attached). Rejoin white with the last yo of the last st. Leave red yarn at the side. Turn.

Row 5: Ch, 2 sk the first 2 dc. Continue working a dc in skipped sts of the two rows below and ch 2 over dc of the last row. Complete the row by working ch 2, sl st in top of turning chain. Change color by drawing new color through the sl st. Turn.

Repeat rows 4 and 5 for pattern, alternating white, blue, and red until desired length, ending with white and pattern Row 5.

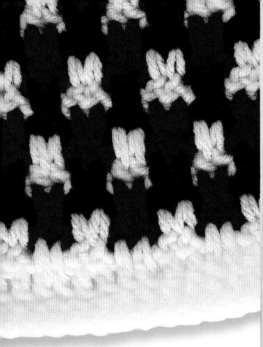

Last row: With white yarn, ch 3, dc in skipped st of two rows below, dc in next 2 dc of last row, dc in each skipped st of two rows below. Continue across row. Complete the row by working dc in skipped st of two rows below and dc in top of turning chain (22 dc).

Finishing: Using white yarn, work sc evenly spaced around the edges and top and bottom, work 3 sc in each corner. Join with sl st. Sl st around entire scarf. Weave in all ends.

C OME NOW, LET
US REASON
TOGETHER.
LYNDON B. JOHNSON

DESIGNER: PENNY COTT

EYEGLASS HOLDER

Even if you've never made a piece of beaded jewelry before, this project is so, so easy. Your local bead store will have all of the materials — the only difficult part will be choosing from hundreds of incredible beads!

WHAT YOU NEED
Flexible beading wire
Wire cutters
2 crimp beads
2 lanyard hooks
Crimping or needle-nose pliers
45 blue and red barrel-shaped beads, 10 mm long
44 brass rondel spacers, 6 mm
2 eyeglass leashes

1 Cut a 26-inch length of flexible beading wire. String a crimp bead onto one end of the wire. Loop the wire through a lanyard hook and back into the crimp bead. Squish the crimp bead with the pliers.

2 String barrel-shaped beads and rondel spacers in an alternating pattern until you have used all of the beads.

3 String a crimp bead onto the other wire end. Loop the wire through the remaining lanyard hook and back into the crimp bead. Check to make sure there aren't any huge gaps in between the beads, then squish the crimp bead.

4 Attach the lanyard hooks to the eyeglass holders.

NEVER BELIEVE THAT A FEW CARING PEOPLE CAN'T CHANGE THE WORLD. FOR, INDEED, THAT'S ALL WHO EVER HAVE.
MARGARET MEAD

DESIGNER: CHRIS RANKIN

STAR-STAMPED SCARF

Don't be fooled by the richness of the embossed velvet or the fine detail of the gold beaded fringe — this luxurious scarf is deceptively easy to make.

DESIGNER: RAIN NEWCOMB

WHAT YOU NEED

½ yard of blue rayon/acetate velvet, 16 inches wide

Ruler

Piece of soap

Scissors

Rubber star stamp

Padded ironing board

Spray bottle

Iron

Needle and thread

Blue cotton/polyester sewing thread

Pressing cloth

Size 12 beading needle

Size D gold bead thread

1 hank of size 11/0 gold-lined seed beads

1 On the back side of the velvet, mark the center using the ruler and the soap. Because velvet is a napped fabric, it is important to sew the pieces with the nap running in the same direction. Brush your hand lightly across the fabric to determine which direction the nap is running. With the nap running down, mark each piece at the top, then cut along the marked line.

2 To emboss the velvet, place your stamp face up on the ironing board. Lay a piece of scrap velvet, right side down, on the face of the stamp. Lightly mist the area of the fabric directly over the stamp with the spray bottle. Turn the iron on a high or cotton setting, and place it on the velvet-covered stamp. Be sure to avoid the steam holes in the iron (they'll leave marks). Press for about 20 seconds. Lift up the iron to make sure you've imprinted the entire stamp.

3 When you're happy with your practice efforts, emboss a scattering of stars on the scarf pieces.

4 Place right sides of the velvet together with the nap running down. Baste ¼ inch from each edge within the seam allowance.

5 Sew a ½-inch seam down one side. With a pressing cloth and a low-heat iron, lightly press the seam allowance to one side. (Note: If the iron is too hot, it will mar the fabric.)

6 Baste the other seam and stitch in the same direction as the first seam (with the nap running down), then press as directed in Step 5.

7 Remove the basting stitches and turn the scarf right side out. Cover the edges with the pressing cloth and lightly press along both sides, taking care not to mar the fabric.

8 Turn each end under ¾ inch. Press lightly, using the pressing cloth, and machine stitch the ends closed with a ⅜-inch top stitching. For a softer finish, hand-stitch the ends closed.

9 To create the beaded fringe, thread the beading needle with beading thread. Double the thread and tie a knot in the end. Beginning on one corner, push the needle through the end of velvet, hiding the knot. String 35 gold beads. Bring the needle up through the rest of the beads, skipping the last bead you put on. Take a small stitch through the velvet, exiting the needle where you want to begin the next fringe. Repeat this process until you have completed the fringe.

PATRIOTIC HAT

This unisex hat is a great weekend knitting project. If you prefer a cap style, just shorten the pattern by an inch.

WHAT YOU NEED

One 100-gram ball each in navy, red and white in Plymouth Yarn Company's Encore worsted weight yarn (75% acrylic, 25% wool)

One set each of double-pointed knitting needles in size 8 and 9 (or sizes needed to obtain correct gauge)

Flag button, optional

GAUGE

20 sts = 4 inches measured over stockinette st with larger needles

SIZE

To fit the average adult head

1 Using red yarn and smaller needles, cast on 100 sts and work in corrugated rib pattern as follows. For row one, k2 red, k2 white, to end of round. Place marker to denote beginning of round.

2 For row two, k2 red, p2 white to end of round. Repeat row two until the corrugated rib measures 2½ inches.

3 Cut red and white yarns. Change to larger needles and navy yarn. Work in stockinette st for 4 inches. Work will measure approx 6½ inches from the beginning.

4 To shape the crown, first decrease row: k8, k2 tog to end of round. Next and every alternate round, knit. For the second decrease row, k7, knit 2 tog to end of round. For the third decrease row, k6, knit 2 tog to end of round. Continue working the decreases in this manner until the final round of k2 tog. Ten sts will remain.

5 Cut yarn. Thread a needle and draw yarn through the remaining sts. Fasten off tightly.

6 To finish, darn in the ends and sew a button on top of hat if desired.

& SCARF

Easy to knit and easy to wear, this scarf will soon become one of your favorites. The rolled edge design decreases bulkiness and makes it look great.

WHAT YOU NEED

2 balls navy, 1 ball red, and 1 ball white of Plymouth Yarn Company's Encore worsted weight yarn (75% acrylic, 25% wool)

Knitting needles in size 10 or size needed to obtain gauge

GAUGE
20 sts = 5 inches
   (4 stitches = 1 inch)
   measured over
   stockinette st

FINISHED
   MEASUREMENTS
Approximately 85 inches
   before knotting the
   ends

1 Cast on 40 sts with navy yarn and work in stockinette st for 14 inches ending with right side facing.

2 Cut blue yarn and join in red. Work 2 rows. Join in white, work 2 rows.

3 Continue in red and white stripes as established for a total of 7 red and 6 white stripes, ending with a red stripe.

4 Rejoin navy yarn and continue in stockinette st for approximately 48 inches. Cut navy yarn.

5 Rejoin red and white yarns and work in stripe pattern as before. Rejoin navy and work a further 14 inches. Bind off loosely.

6 To finish, darn in yarn ends, then tie a knot at each end of scarf just below the stripes.

DESIGNER: CATHERINE HAM

PATRIOTIC SWEATER

This loose, comfortable sweater design is a great way to show your patriotic colors. If you prefer a sweater over a tunic, just make it shorter.

WHAT YOU NEED

6 (6, 6, 7, 7) balls navy, 1 (1, 1, 1, 1) ball red, and 1 (1, 1, 1, 1) ball white in Plymouth Yarn Company's Encore worsted weight yarn (75% acrylic, 25% wool)

Knitting needles in sizes 9 and 8 or size needed to obtain gauge

Small flag applique, optional

GAUGE

18 sts and 24 rows = 4 inches measured over St st with larger needles

SIZES

Extra small (small, medium, large, extra large)

FINISHED MEASURE-MENTS

Bust: 39 (41, 43, 45, 47) inches

Length: 28 (28½, 29, 30, 30½) inches

Sleeve length: 18 (18½, 18½, 19, 19) inches

BACK

With smaller needles and red, cast on 90 (94, 98, 102, 106) sts.

Row 1: (k2 red, k2 white), to last 2 sts, k2 red

Row 2: (p2 red, k2 white), to last 2 sts, p2 red

Row 3: (k2 red, p2 white), to last 2 sts, k2 red

These rows establish the corrugated rib pattern. Repeat rows 2 and 3 until the rib measures 2 inches for all sizes, ending with right side facing. Be careful to strand the yarn loosely when changing color.

Change to larger needles and navy yarn and continue in St st, decreasing 1st at each side for first and second sizes only. (88, 92, 98, 102, 106) sts.

Continue in St st until work measures 16 (16½, 16½, 17, 17) inches or desired length. Shape underarm: BO 4 (4, 5, 7, 7) sts at beg. of next two rows. When work measures 26½ (27, 27½, 28½, 29) inches, shape back neck: with right side facing, knit 28 (30, 31, 31, 32) sts. Place rest of sts on holder. Decrease 1 st at neck edge on next and every alternate row, 3 times. Knit until work measures 28 (28½, 29, 30, 30½) inches. BO the 25 (27, 28, 28, 29) shoulder sts. Return to sts on holder. Knit across 24 (24, 26, 26, 28) sts and place these on holder for center back neck. Continue on remaining sts and work to correspond with the first side.

FRONT

Work as given for back until the work measures 25 (25½, 26, 27, 27½) inches. Begin neck shaping: With right side facing, knit 31 (33, 35, 35, 35) sts and place rest of sts on a holder. Decrease 1 st at neck edge every alternate row until 25 (27, 28, 28, 29) sts remain. Work straight until the piece measures the same as the back. BO the shoulder sts. Return to the sts on the holder, leave center 18 (18, 18, 18,

NECKBAND

Using smaller needles and navy yarn, with right side facing, pick up and knit approximately 84 (86, 88, 90, 92) sts around neck edge, including sts left on holders. Check that you have picked up sts evenly.

Work in k1, p1 rib for an inch. Bind off loosely in rib. Sew shoulder and neckband seams neatly.

Sew sleeves in place. Sew up side and sleeve seams, taking care to match seams at the corrugated ribbing. Darn in yarn ends.

If desired, add a flag applique at the sleeve edge or at one side just above the ribbing.

22) sts on holder, rejoin yarn to the remaining sts and work decreases at neck edge as before. Complete to match the first side.

SLEEVE

Using smaller needles, and red, cast on 38 (42, 42, 46, 46) sts and work in corrugated rib pattern as given for the BACK until the rib measures 2½ inches for all sizes. Change to larger needles and navy yarn and continue working in St st, increasing one stitch at each end of the next and every following 3rd row until there are 86 (86, 90, 94, 100) sts. Continue knitting until sleeve measures 18 (18½, 18½, 19, 19) inches. BO loosely.

FINISHING

Seam one shoulder together.

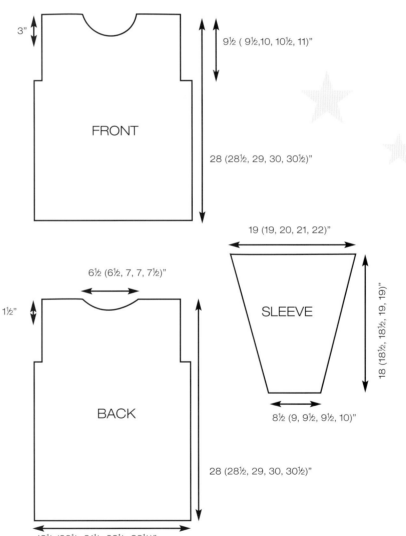

FRONT

3"

9½ (9½,10, 10½, 11)"

28 (28½, 29, 30, 30½)"

6½ (6½, 7, 7, 7½)"

1½"

BACK

28 (28½, 29, 30, 30½)"

19½ (20½, 21½, 22½, 23½)"

19 (19, 20, 21, 22)"

SLEEVE

18 (18½, 18½, 19, 19)"

8½ (9, 9½, 9½, 10)"

STAR SPANGLED EARRINGS

A quick trip to your favorite bead store will provide all the inspiration (and materials!) needed for these easy-to-make earrings. For a slightly more challenging project, try using several head pins of varying lengths to create a cascade of stars and stripes.

WHAT YOU NEED
4 2-inch sterling silver head pins
2 sterling silver jump rings
2 sterling silver French ear wires
4 red star beads
Blue and white seed beads
Round-nose pliers
Wire cutters

1 Slide one blue and one white seed bead and a red star bead onto each of the silver head pins.

2 On two of the head pins, add 8 to 10 seed beads, alternating colors. Add 12 to 14 seed beads to the remaining two head pins, alternating colors.

3 Using wire cutters, trim the wire at the top of the head pins to ¼ inch above the last bead.

4 Make a three-quarter loop at the top of each head pin using the round-nose pliers, then attach one short and one long beaded head pin to each jump ring. Use the round-nose pliers to close the loops.

5 Slightly open the loop on the French ear wires with the pliers. Attach a jump ring to each ear wire, and securely close the loop.

DESIGNER: TRACY HILDEBRAND

DESIGNER: JOAN K. MORRIS

STARS & STRIPES T-SHIRT

This bandanna-inspired T-shirt is simple to make and looks great with denim. While you're working, consider cutting out a few extra stars and stripes to add to your favorite jean jacket or vest.

WHAT YOU NEED
Navy blue T-shirt
2 bandannas, one white and one red
1 yard iron-on adhesive
Red fabric paint with a fine-tip applicator, optional

1 Prewash the T-shirt and bandannas. Apply the iron-on adhesive to the wrong side of the white and the red bandannas, referring to the manufacturer's instructions.

2 Cut out three stars and the letters from the white bandanna using the patterns on page 117.

3 Cut out three 1½- x 12-inch rectangles from the red bandanna. (Tip: The corners tend to have the more pleasing patterns.)

4 Place the T-shirt on the ironing board and arrange your appliques, using the photo as a guide. Apply the appliques with an iron, referring to the manufacturer's instructions. If desired, outline the design elements with a fine layer of fabric paint.

THE ESSENCE OF DEMOCRACY IS ITS ASSURANCE THAT EVERY HUMAN BEING SHOULD SO RESPECT HIMSELF AND SHOULD BE SO RESPECTED IN HIS OWN PERSONALITY THAT HE SHOULD HAVE OPPORTUNITY EQUAL TO THAT OF EVERY OTHER HUMAN BEING TO SHOW WHAT HE WAS MEANT TO BECOME.

ANNA GARLIN SPENCER

STREAMING STARS BERET

Feeling tres chic? Transform a purchased beret with a few simple craft store items in less than an hour. For added drama, trail a few ribbons off the back of this hat.

WHAT YOU NEED

½ yard each of ¼-inch red and white satin ribbon
¼ yard iron-on adhesive
Navy blue beret
Hand towel
3 star appliques with adhesive backing
10 gold star studs and stud applicator

1 Cut three 7-inch lengths of red and white ribbon. Apply iron-on adhesive to the wrong side of the cut ribbon pieces, referring to the manufacturer's instructions.

2 Loosely fill the beret with a hand towel to give it the proper shape. Pin the star appliques onto the top left quadrant of the beret, placing them evenly around the curve of the beret.

3 Position a length of red ribbon on the upper inside point of the top star applique and a white ribbon on the lower inside point of the top star applique. Position lengths of red and white ribbon on the middle and bottom star appliques.

4 Trim the ribbon ends at angles so they're flush with the edges of the appliques, then trim the ribbon lengths to follow the curve of the beret, approximately 1 inch from the edge.

5 Iron the star appliques and ribbons onto the beret, referring to the manufacturer's instructions. (Note: If the appliques don't adhere well, secure them in place by hand with gold thread.)

6 Place a star stud at the end of each ribbon, and scatter the remaining studs around the beret for a total of 13, referring to the manufacturer's instructions.

DESIGNER: JOAN K. MORRIS

DESIGNER: JOAN K. MORRIS

TOTE BAG

This roomy, patriotic carryall is great for all of your everyday gear. Take it to the gym, on picnics, and to the library. For a matching T-shirt or jean jacket, just repeat the instructions below using narrower ribbon.

1 Measure and cut four 10-inch lengths and three 16-inch lengths of red ribbon.

2 Measure and cut six 6-inch lengths of the blue ribbon, and six 6-inch lengths from the white ribbon.

3 Following the manufacturer's instructions, apply the iron-on adhesive to one side of all ribbon lengths.

4 Working on a flat surface (an ironing board is ideal), position all six blue ribbon pieces horizontally on the upper left corner of the tote bag with their side edges touching.

5 Starting on the left side, vertically weave a length of white ribbon through the horizontal layers of blue ribbon. Repeat this process with the five remaining white ribbons, alternating the weave of the ribbon. Once all the ribbons are woven, adjust them as needed so there is no space between them.

6 Position one of the 10-inch red ribbons horizontally on the tote bag, aligning its top edge with the top edge of the blue and white square. Position a second 10-inch length of red ribbon at the bottom edge of the woven ribbon square and center the remaining two 10-inch red ribbons in the space between the top and bottom red ribbons.

7 Position the three 16-inch red ribbons in the space below the section assembled in Steps 4-6, allowing the same amount of space between ribbons.

8 Secure the ribbons in place with a hot iron as directed in the iron-on adhesive manufacturer's instructions.

THERE IS DANGER FROM ALL MEN. THE ONLY MAXIM OF A FREE GOVERNMENT OUGHT TO BE TO TRUST NO MAN LIVING WITH POWER TO ENDANGER THE PUBLIC LIBERTY.

JOHN ADAMS

QUICK & EASY CROCHET HAT

Simple stripes and a single star add pizazz to this easy-to-make crocheted hat. The colors can be mixed and matched for interesting variations.

ABBREVIATIONS
hd = half double
sc = single crochet
tr = treble crochet
ch = chain
sl st = slip stitch
st = stitch
yo = yarn over
* repeat instructions between asterisks the number of times indicated

SIZES
Small (Medium, Large)

GAUGE
3 hd = 1 inch using double strands of yarn

WHAT YOU NEED
5 ounces (6, 7) white 4-ply yarn
Less than an ounce each of red and blue worsted weight
Size H hook
Tapestry needle
Stitch marker

STAR

Wrap the blue yarn around your finger 7 times to form a ring and sl st in ring to secure.

Round 1: Ch 4, 4 tr in ring, *ch 2, 5 tr in ring.* Repeat 4 times. Ch 2, join with a sl st to 4th st of ch 4. Do not turn at end of rounds.

Round 2: Ch 4, leaving last loop of each tr on hook. Work 1 tr in each of the next 4 tr, yo and draw through all 5 loops on hook (cluster formed). Ch 3, sl st into 1st sc (picot formed). Ch 4 sl st in ch 2 space (1st point of star formed). *Ch 4, leaving last loop of each tr on back with 1 tr in each of the next 5 tr, yo, and draw through all 6 loops on hook, make picot, ch 4, sl st into ch 2 space* 3 more times. Ch 4, sl st into ch 2 space. Ch 4, sl st in sc of 1st picot. End, leaving long thread for sewing star to crown of hat.

CROWN

Using 2 strands of white yarn, ch 2, 8 sc in 2nd ch from hook, join with sl st to 1st sc (mark beginning of round).

Round 1: Ch 2, hd in same st as sl st, 2 hd in each of next 7 sts, join with sl st to top of ch 2 (16 hd with ch 2 counting as 1 hd).

Round 2: Ch 2, hd in same st as sl st. * hd in next st, 2 hd in next st. * Repeat around, ending with hd in last s. Join with sl st (24 sts).

Round 3: Ch 2, hd in same st as sl st.* hd in next 2 sts, 2 hd in next st.* Repeat around, ending with hd in last st. Join with sl st (32 sts).

Round 4: Ch 2, hd in same st as sl st.* hd in each of next 3 sts, 2 hd in next st. *Repeat around, ending with hd in each of last 3 sts. Join round with sl st (40 sts).

DESIGNER: PENNY COTT

Rounds 5-7: Continue increasing in this manner for 3 more rounds (64 sts). Stop here for small size, but do not cut yarn. Sew star to crown of hat, then proceed to turning chain.

Round 8 (for medium size only): Ch 2, hd in same st as sl st. * hd in each of next 15 sts, 2 hd in next st. * Repeat around, ending with hd in each of last 15 sts. Join yarn with sl st (68 sts). Stop here for medium size, but do not cut yarn. Sew star to crown of hat, then proceed to turning chain.

Round 9 (for large size only): Ch 2, hd in same st as sl st, * hd in each of next 7 sts, 2 hd in next st.* Repeat around, ending with hd in each of last 7 sts. Join round with sl st (72 sts). Sew star to crown of hat, then proceed to turning chain.

Turning Chain: Working into front loop only of last round, sl st in each stitch around. Join with a sl st to the back loop of the st you worked 1st in this round.

SIDE

Round 1: Working in back loop only of same round, ch 2, hd in each st around. Join with a sl st to 2nd chain of ch 2 64 (68, 72) sts.

Round 2: Ch 2, hd in each st around. Join as in Round 1.

Round 3: Repeat Round 2 five times.

Finishing Round: Sl st in each st around. Cut yarn and fasten off. Work in all ends.

OVERLAY CHAIN FOR STRIPES
(around side of hat)

Attach red yarn with a sl st around the post of a hd at the back of hat on Row 6. Sc around each hd past on this round. Do not join. Cut yarn and fasten off. Repeat this stripe on Round 4 and Round 2 of the side of the hat. (Tip: This process is easiest if the crown is facing you.) Carefully work in all ends.

IT IS THE FLAG JUST AS MUCH OF THE MAN WHO WAS NATURALIZED YESTERDAY AS OF THE MAN WHOSE PEOPLE HAVE BEEN HERE MANY GENERATIONS.

HENRY CABOT LODGE

NIGHT SHIRT

Climb into bed under the stars in this easy-to-make night shirt.

WHAT YOU NEED
Navy blue T-shirt, pre-washed
Cardboard or poster board
Spray adhesive
Bandanna or fabric with red and white striped design
Fabric paint in red, white, and blue
Fine-tip applicator for fabric paint
Small paintbrush
¼ yard iron-on adhesive
2 star-shaped fabric stamps

1 Cut the cardboard to fit between the layers of the T-shirt. Spray one side of the cardboard with spray adhesive and carefully place it inside the T-shirt, adhesive side up. Smooth any wrinkles in the fabric.

2 Using the templates on page 119, cut a crescent moon shape out of the bandanna. Following the manufacturer's instructions, apply

DESIGNER: JOAN K. MORRIS

the iron-on adhesive to the wrong side of the fabric moon.

3 Prepare the white fabric paint as directed by the manufacturer. Pour a small amount of paint onto a plate or other palette. Practice using the star stamp and the white paint on a piece of scrap fabric until you are comfortable and pleased with the results. Stamp a pleasing pattern of stars on the upper left side of the shirt, combining large and small stars. If any stamp area is not sufficiently cov-

ered with paint, use a brush to fill it in. Let paint completely dry.

4 Practice using the fine-tip applicator on the bottle of white fabric paint, then outline each star. Let dry.

5 With the fine tip attached to the bottle of red fabric paint, practice writing on scrap fabric. Once you are comfortable and pleased with the results, write "by the dawn's early light" underneath the stars, leaving room for the crescent moon.

6 Following the manufacturer's instructions and with the cardboard still inside the shirt, iron the crescent moon to the right side of the shirt. Outline the moon with blue fabric paint and the fine-tip applicator.

7 Wait at least seven days to wash the T-shirt. Wash it inside out and dry without heat.

SEED BEAD NECKLACES

DESIGNER: CHRIS RANKIN

You'll be amazed at the number of pattern variations you can create with only three bead colors. Wear the necklaces one at a time, or make several in varying lengths and wear them together.

WHAT YOU NEED
Size 12 beading needle
Size D beading thread
Seed beads of your choice
Clasp
Clear nail polish with nylon

1 Thread the needle with beading thread. Double the thread and tie a knot in the end.

2 Thread five seed beads, leaving a 5-inch tail on the end.

3 Pass the beads through one end of the clasp. Go back through the seed beads you just put on, starting with the bead closest to the tail.

78

4 Pull the thread tight to create a loop of seed beads that hold the clasp.

5 String the seed beads in a pleasing pattern until your necklace is the desired length.

Repeat Steps 2 through 4 (but don't leave a tail) to attach the other end of the clasp. Pass through the seed bead loop twice, then go through a few beads in the necklace.

6 Brush nail polish onto the last ¾ inch of the thread next to the beads. Pass through 1 inch of the beads strung. (The nail polish will cement the thread to itself inside of the beads, holding the necklace together.) Trim the thread.

7 Thread both pieces of the tail into a needle. (If you find threading both pieces difficult, do them one at a time.) Repeat Step 6 to secure these ends.

I STARTED WITH THIS IDEA IN MY HEAD, "THERE'S TWO THINGS I'VE GOT A RIGHT TO...DEATH OR LIBERTY".
HARRIET TUBMAN

OLD GLORY KEY CHAIN

What better way to show off you patriotic pride than by attaching colorful beads to your key chain? This project is incredibly easy, making it an ideal quick gift for special occasions.

WHAT YOU NEED
Length of red suede lace, 3½ inches long
2 lengths of white suede lace, each 3 inches long
3 large chevron beads
Key chain

1 Thread one chevron onto each of the pieces of suede lace, then tie a knot at the bottom.

2 Tie the top of the red suede lace to the key chain. Position the white laces on either side and adjust the length until the beads hang where you want them. Tie a knot in the top of each one.

3 Trim the knots and add a set of keys.

DESIGNER: CHRIS RANKIN

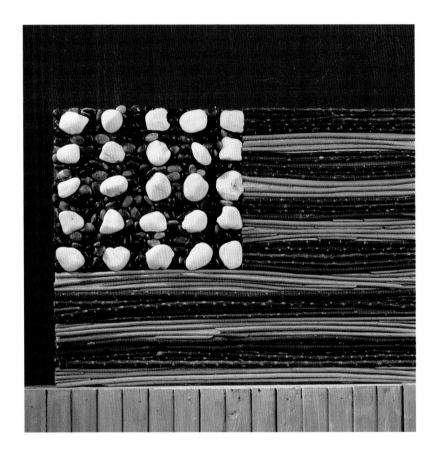

W HY HAS GOVERNMENT BEEN INSTITUTED AT
ALL? BECAUSE THE PASSIONS OF MEN WILL NOT
CONFORM TO THE DICTATES OF REASON AND JUSTICE
WITHOUT CONSTRAINT.

ALEXANDER HAMILTON

OUTDOORS

Decorating the great outdoors in red, white, and blue is a great way to show your national pride while adding color and style to your neighborhood.

Most of the projects in this book are both decorative and functional. The crackled flower pots and star window box (pages 90 and 100), for example, make great containers for bright red flowers, while the lanterns and luminaria (pages 85, 96, and 102) are fun types of outdoor lighting.

Don't let your imagination stop with the projects in this chapter. Many of the techniques used in this book can be used to create one-of-a-kind outdoor displays. The layered painting technique used to create the special effects on the Mists of American photo frame on page 17, for example, can easily be adapted to create embellish an old picnic table, flower pots, or even your driveway!

RUSTIC FLAG

Create your own rustic flag with twigs and stones from your backyard. Nature walks and hikes can also provide an interesting variety of inspiring materials.

WHAT YOU NEED

Sticks

24 x 18 inch sheet of ¼- or ½-inch plywood

Gesso

Flat brush

Red, white, and blue acrylic paint

Red and white sticks about ¼ inch or smaller in diameter

White rocks about 1 inch in diameter

Small pebbles

Hedge pruners

Glue gun and glue

Spray polyurethane

1 Prepare the board with a heavy coat of gesso. After the gesso dries, mark off the star and stripe areas with a pencil, referring to the illustration as a guide.

2 Paint the stripes red and white, then paint the rectangle solid blue. Allow the paint to dry completely.

3 Arrange and hot-glue the red and white sticks to the striped areas, piecing them together as you would a mosaic. Designer tip: Cut the sticks at an angle so they will blend together when you position them end to end.

4 Arrange and hot glue the large white rocks in place, then fill in with the smaller rocks.

5 Trim off any protruding twigs with the pruners.

6 Apply several coats of spray polyurethane to the flag if you plan to display it outdoors, allowing each coat to dry completely before adding the next.

DESIGNER: DANA IRWIN

PATRIOT LANTERN

This lantern makes a great Saturday afternoon project, even if you're a novice mosaic crafter. The blend of textured and smooth glass creates a great effect in this lantern, but feel free to use just smooth glass if you're trying to keep costs down.

WHAT YOU NEED

Small lantern (8 inches tall x 4 inches wide)

Fine-point permanent marker

Safety glasses

6-inch square sheet each of red, white, and blue stained glass

Glass mosaic cutter nippers

Clear silicone glue

Craft stick

1-inch-wide masking tape

2 small plastic buckets or containers (1- to 3-quart size)

Acrylic/latex fortifier

1 pound white sanded grout

Sponge

Dust mask

Latex or rubber gloves

Razor blade, dental pick, or any small, pointed metal object that can be used as a tool

Soft cloth

1 Photocopy the star and circle patterns on page 120. Trace the circle shape lightly onto the four lantern panels with a permanent marker, then trace the star pattern inside the circles. Designer tip: Rotate the star pattern slightly each time you trace it to create visual interest.

2 Wearing safety glasses, use the glass mosaic cutters to nip and cut the glass into small pieces, keeping the colors separate by cutting each color over a separate paper plate. Vary the sizes of the glass shapes as much as possible to make the finished mosaic more interesting.

TILING THE LANTERN

3 To tile a panel, spread an even layer of glue onto one section of a panel (the star area, for example) with a craft stick. The glue should be thick enough to hold a glass shard securely but not so thick that glue will squeeze up between the pieces. Next, begin placing the glass shards, trying to keep the space between the shards as consistent as possible (approximately ⅛ inch is best for this project). Nip and shape the shards as necessary for a good fit. Designer tip: Try to keep your fingertips free of adhesive as you work to minimize cleanup time.

4 Starting on the front door panel, tile the star in red, the circle in blue, and the background in clear glass, nipping and shaping the pieces as necessary.

5 Turn the lantern to the next panel and mosaic the star in clear glass, the circle in blue, and the background in red. Rest the lantern in your lap or on an old towel while you work.

6 For the third panel, mosaic the star in red glass, the circle in clear glass, and the background in blue. For the fourth panel, mosaic the star in blue, the circle in red, and the background in clear glass. Allow the lantern to dry overnight.

7 Remove any dried glue from the glass surface of the panels with a razor blade or dental pick.

GROUTING THE LANTERN

8 Carefully tape off the metal frame around each of the glass panels. Position the edge of the tape right up to but not over the edge onto the glass. Also tape the hood and the base of the lantern.

9 Fill a plastic container with water and cover your work surface with a protective layer of newspaper. In the second container (wearing the dust mask and gloves) pour small amounts (1 to 2 ounces) of latex fortifier at a time into the pound of grout and mix until the grout is the consistency of thick oatmeal.

10 Working on one panel at a time, use your fingertips to carefully work the grout down in and around all the crevices and along the outer edges of the mosaic.

DESIGNER: JILL MACKAY

11 Wipe the excess grout from the surface of all four panels with a damp sponge. Be careful not to wipe away too much of the grout or you'll end up removing the grout that is between the shards. (If this happens, just reapply more.)

12 Allow the lantern to sit undisturbed for 15 minutes or until it "glazes over." The grout will lighten slightly during this time.

13 With a soft cloth, polish away the hazy appearance left by the grout on your glass. You may need to use a razor blade or dental pick to clean away any dried, stubborn grout, especially from textured glass.

14 When finished cleaning, carefully remove the masking tape and smooth the grout somewhat by running your finger down the outer edge. Repair any damaged grout by reapplying tiny amounts where needed and smoothing again. When finished, wrap in plastic or kraft paper and allow the grout to dry slowly (cure) for three to five days.

PATRIOTIC PINWHEEL

For many of us, colorful pinwheels and summer breezes are a fond part of our childhood memories. This pinwheel is an easy project, even if you're not much of a painter. Consider making smaller versions from stiff paper for indoor decorating.

IGNER: DIANA LIGHT

WHAT YOU NEED
Purchased metal pinwheel
Latex primer
Acrylic paint in red, white, and blue
Wide and fine brushes
Pencil and masking tape
Clear enamel finishing spray

1 Prepare the pinwheel's surface by painting it with two coats of primer.

2 Working on the back side of the pinwheel, paint two opposite panels blue and two opposite panels red. Allow the paint to dry completely, then paint the front sides of these sections.

3 Working on the front side, paint two opposite corners blue. (Choose the corners whose back sides are red.) After the paint has completely dried, use one of the star templates in the back of the book to transfer a star shape on top of the blue. Paint the stars white.

4 Working on the front side, divide the surface area of the two remaining sections into four stripes and lightly mark them with a pencil. Paint the stripes red and white, using masking tape to ensure straight lines and allowing the paint to dry completely between colors.

5 After the paint has completely dried, finish with a coat of clear enamel spray.

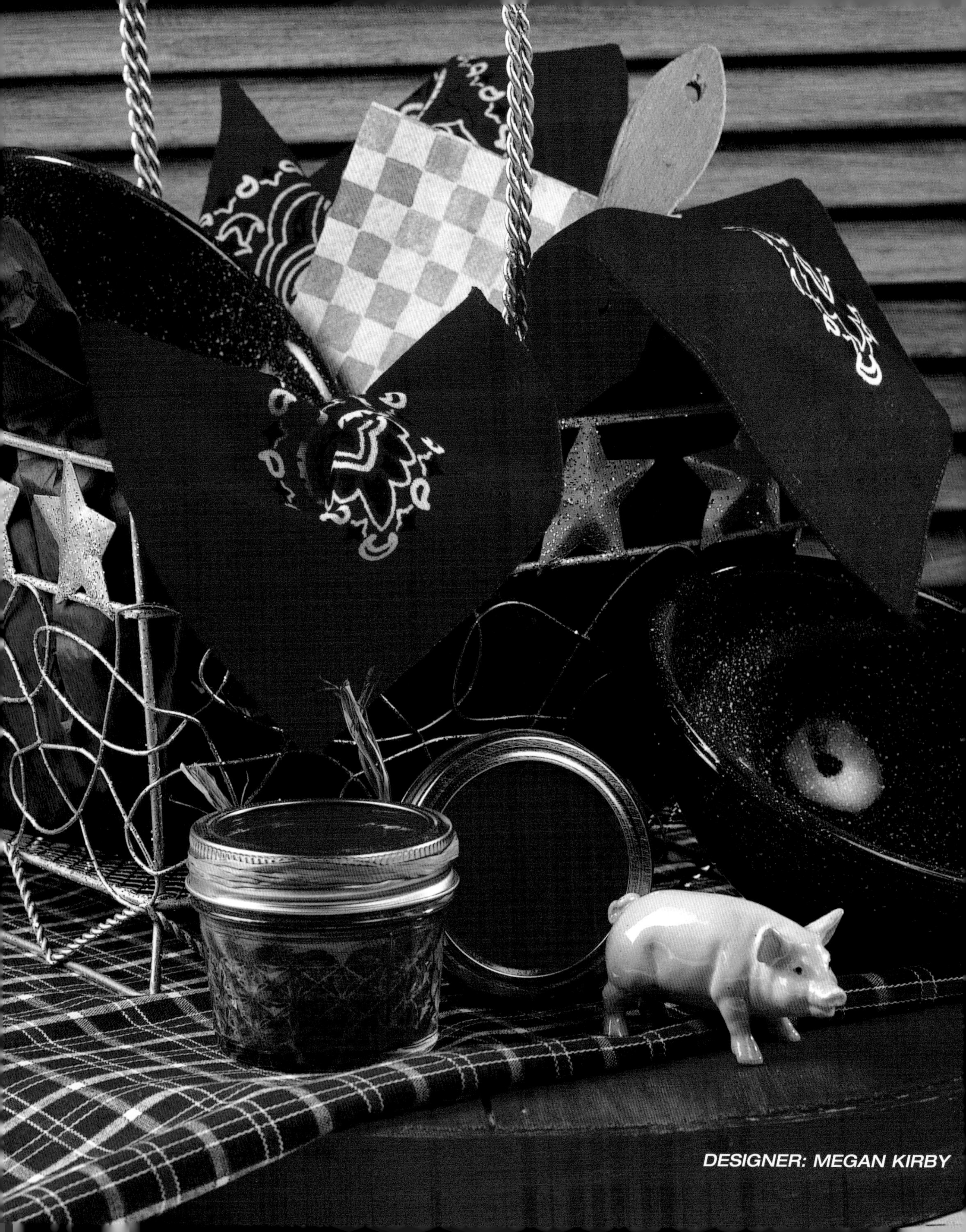

DESIGNER: MEGAN KIRBY

BARBECUE GIFT BASKET

Gift baskets are a great way to say thank you in your own unique way. Fill the spice jars with individual or blended spices, and be sure to include your favorite recipes.

WHAT YOU NEED
Blue tissue paper
Festive basket
Red bandanna
Gift card
Chili bowls
Stirring spoon
Favorite chili recipe
Spices from recipe
Red raffia

1 Layer the tissue paper on the bottom of the basket, then arrange the bandanna on top of it.

2 Write your favorite chili recipe on the gift card and decorate the spice containers with red raffia.

3 Arrange the chili bowls, serving spoon, and spices inside the basket. Fluff the bandanna and tissue paper if necessary to create a more pleasing appearance, then place the gift card in a prominent position.

HE SERVES HIS PARTY BEST WHO SERVES HIS COUNTRY BEST.
RUTHERFORD B HAYES

OUR FAVORITES!

CHILI SPICE MIX
2 T all-purpose flour
1 t dried red pepper
4 T instant minced onion
1 t instant minced garlic
3 t chili powder
1 t sugar
2 t seasoned salt
1 t ground cumin

TO MAKE CHILI
Brown 1 lb ground beef. Drain. Add 2 cans kidney beans, 2 cans tomatoes and ¼ cup chili spice mix. Reduce heat and simmer 10 minutes, stirring occasionally. Makes 4 to 6 servings.

BARBECUE RUB MIX
8 T brown sugar
2 T salt
2 T oregano
2 T cumin
4 T garlic powder
4 T chili powder
4 T paprika
2 T onion powder
4 T dry mustard
½ t cayenne

TO MAKE BARBECUE
This barbeque rub is great for all meats. Just rub it into the meat and allow to sit for one hour before grilling.

COLONIAL FLOWERPOTS

A simple coat of crackle glaze (available in craft supply stores) transforms an ordinary blue pot into a Colonial-style container that's perfect for showcasing displays of red and white blooming plants.

WHAT YOU NEED
Terra-cotta pot(s)
Paintbrush
Water-based sealant
Flat blue latex paint
Crackle glaze
Transparent glaze
Foam brush or sponge
Cotton cloth

1 Clean the pot well and allow it to dry completely. Apply a coat of water-based sealant to both the inside and outside of the pot. Allow to dry overnight.

2 Paint the outside of the pot with blue paint. Allow to dry overnight. Apply a second coat if needed.

3 Apply a coat of crackle glaze over the outer surface with a foam brush or sponge. Let dry overnight.

4 Apply a coat of transparent glaze with a cotton cloth, then use a clean section of the cloth to wipe away any excess glaze. Allow to dry overnight.

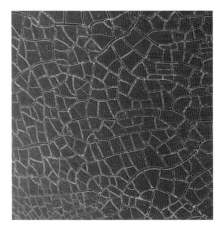

Designer Tip: it's easy to vary the look of these pots by reversing or subtituting colors. Try white paint with a blue glaze or red paint with white glaze.

D EMOCRACY CANNOT BE SAVED BY SUPERMEN, BUT ONLY BY THE UNSWERVING DEVOTION AND GOODNESS OF MILLIONS OF LITTLE MEN

ADLAI EWING STEVENSON

DESIGNER: MEGAN KIRBY

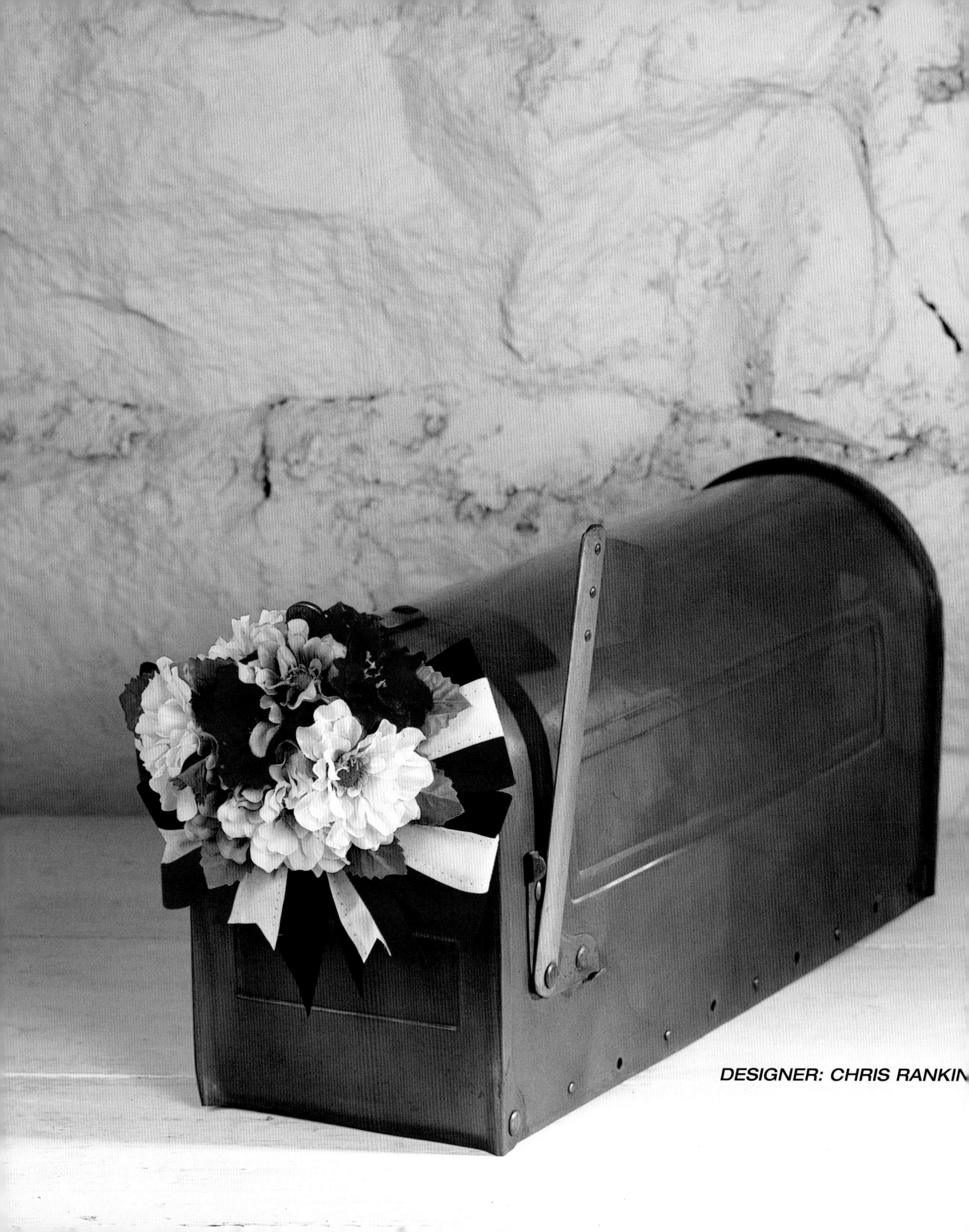

DESIGNER: CHRIS RANKIN

MAILBOX CORSAGE

Mailboxes make a great place to display a hint of red, white, and blue. This corsage is easy to assemble, and the silk flowers will weather the elements in style.

WHAT YOU NEED

7 medium-sized silk flowers in red, white, and blue (zinnias were used here)

Vinyl-backed bow

Floral wire

Green floral tape

Wire cutters

Sharp scissors

1 Trim the flower stems 5 inches from the blossoms with wire cutters. If your flowers have leaves, push them up the stems so they rest under the blooms.

2 Hold the flower stems together to form a very tight bouquet, then secure them together by wrapping with floral wire.

3 Wrap the stems with floral tape, wrapping at an angle and stretching the tape slightly as you work.

4 Fold a 14-inch length of floral wire in half and wind it around the center of the bow.

Place your bouquet on top of the bow and secure it in place by winding the wire around the bouquet. Use the remaining wire to create a loop to attach the corsage to your mailbox.

5 Create a swallow-tail effect on the ends of the bow's ribbon by folding the ribbon ends in half and cutting on a 45-degree angle with sharp scissors.

NOTHING IN THIS WORLD CAN TAKE THE PLACE OF PERSISTENCE. TALENT WILL NOT; NOTHING IS MORE COMMON THAN UNSUCCESSFUL PEOPLE WITH TALENT. GENIUS WILL NOT; UNREWARDED GENIUS IS ALMOST A PROVERB. EDUCATION WILL NOT; THE WORLD IS FULL OF EDUCATED DERELICTS. PERSISTENCE AND DETERMINATION ALONE ARE OMNIPOTENT. THE SLOGAN 'PRESS ON' HAS SOLVED AND ALWAYS WILL SOLVE THE PROBLEMS OF THE HUMAN RACE.

CALVIN COOLIDGE

PATRIOTIC BIRDHOUSE

Perk up an ordinary wood birdhouse (available in most large craft stores) with patriotic colors and designs. The washed effect is easy to do and creates a more natural look.

WHAT YOU NEED

Unfinished wood birdhouse

Watercolor paints in white, cobalt blue, and cadmium red

Palette

2 natural hair paintbrushes, one ⅛-inch round and one ¼-inch round

Star stencils, one large enough to fit around the center opening and a second one about half the size, optional

1 Working freehand or with a stencil, outline a large star shape around the opening of the birdhouse with a pencil. Lightly outline several smaller stars on the sides of the house.

2 Paint the stars with the smaller brush and white paint diluted with just a little water. Next, paint the perch and base white. Allow paint to dry completely.

3 Mix enough water with some blue paint to create a wash effect and paint the sides, front, and back of the birdhouse blue. Allow most of the paint to dry completely, then use a dry paper towel to blot up any remaining wet paint.

4 Use a dampened paper towel to blot off any blue paint in the star areas. When dry, paint a second white coat over the stars and allow to dry.

5 Mix enough water with some red paint to create a wash effect and paint the roof with the large brush. Repeat the toweling process from Step 3.

I SWEAR TO THE LORD
I STILL CAN'T SEE WHY
DEMOCRACY MEANS
EVERYBODY BUT ME.
LANGSTON HUGHES

DESIGNER: DIANA LIGHT

DESIGNER: KATHLEEN TRENCHARD

STATUE OF LIBERTY LUMINARIA

Transform an ordinary paper bag into a Lady Liberty luminaria to decorate your front porch or serve as a table centerpiece. The technique is simple and can be mastered in minutes.

WHAT YOU NEED

2 standard-size paper bags with flat bottoms, coated red and/or blue

7 paper clips

Pointed tool such as an awl or sharp pointed nail

Hammer

Scissors

Block of wood or heavy plastic to protect work surface

1 Enlarge the pattern on page 121 as directed and cut to fit the bag. Flatten the bags and fold their bottoms down, holding the folds down with paper clips. Stack the bags one on top of the other.

2 Attach the pattern to the paper bags on all four sides with paper clips. Make sure that the pattern is centered and the image does not cover the folded-down bottom flaps. Move the pattern up if necessary.

3 Punch out the image following the dots of the pattern.

4 Using scissors, cut the top scallop border, according to the pattern.

5 Gently remove the clips, separate the bags, and open them completely. You will notice two new punched designs on the sides of the bags. These designs are open to interpretation.

6 To light the luminarias, put sand or pebbles in the bottom of the bags. Place a votive candle in a glass candleholder in the center of the bottom of the bag. Use a long match to light the candle and keep away from wind or rain.

FRONT DOOR WREATH

French ribbon, also known as wired ribbon, makes a great choice for outdoor craft projects. Curve it gently around a natural vine base, add a few silk flowers, and you'll have a great wreath in minutes.

WHAT YOU NEED
Large vine wreath base
2 pipe cleaners
10 to 12 stalks of wheat
Wire ribbon
Silk greenery
White or ivory silk flowers
Assortment of small red and
 blue accent silks
Glue gun

1 Arrange the wheat stalks into a bouquet and secure them about an inch from their base with the pipe cleaner. Position the wheat bouquet at an angle and secure it to the base by twisting the ends of the pipe cleaner.

2 Tie the ribbon into a bow. Hot-glue the center of the bow over the wheat stems, then curve the ribbon streamers around the sides of the wreath.

3 Arrange the silk greenery down the sides of the wreath, then attach by adding hot glue to the stems and inserting them into the vine under the bow. Repeat with the white flowers.

4 Arrange and hot-glue the accent flowers around the sides of the wreath.

5 Insert a pipe cleaner into the back of the wreath vines and twist to create a hanger.

ALL I WANT IS THE SAME THING YOU WANT. TO HAVE A NATION WITH A GOVERNMENT THAT IS AS GOOD AND HONEST AND DECENT AND COMPETENT AND COMPASSIONATE AND AS FILLED WITH LOVE AS ARE THE AMERICAN PEOPLE.

JIMMY CARTER

DESIGNER: CYNTHIA GILLOOLY

PATRIOTIC WINDOW BOX

Reminiscent of the patriotic gardens of World War II, this window box garden features geraniums and ivy. The project is created from a purchased garden box, so no hammering is required, just an afternoon with a paintbrush.

WHAT YOU NEED
Premade window box, preferably cedar
Sandpaper
White acrylic paint, flat or semigloss
Brush
Wood star cutouts
Red or blue acrylic paint
Wood glue
Potting soil
Blooming plants of your choice

---

1 Sand the box to remove all rough areas. Paint the outside of the box with two coats of white paint. Allow to dry completely.

2 Paint the stars red or blue. Allow paint to dry completely, then attach the stars to the window box with wood glue and allow to dry.

3 Fill the box three-fourths full with potting soil. Arrange plants in soil and water thoroughly.

DESIGNER: MEGAN KIRBY

DESIGNER: DIANA LIGHT

PAINTED HURRICANE LAMP

Simple glass hurricane lamps can be found in most large craft stores. They're easy to paint, and the designs look great when illuminated with candle light.

WHAT YOU NEED

Glass hurricane lamp
Small round brush
Gold outliner tube glass paint
Red oven-bake transparent paint
White oven-bake semi-translucent glass paint
Blue oven-bake matte glass paint
Cotton swabs

1 Wash and dry the hurricane glass. Practice drawing a few stars on a scrap piece of paper with the gold tube paint until you are comfortable with the look of the stars and the flow of the paint. (If you prefer, use one of the star templates in the back of the book.) Designer tip: Start each star with the tip to the surface, then lift the tip off the paper (or glass) about ¼ inch. Squeezing gently, let the line fall on the glass. When you're ready to stop, touch the tip to the surface, then quickly lift it straight off.

2 Draw several stars around the hurricane in varying sizes and placement with the gold paint. Allow to dry completely.

3 Referring to the photo as a guide, apply the stripe lines with the gold paint, starting at one end of the hurricane and spiraling up and around, breaking the lines at the stars. Allow to dry completely.

4 Fill in the spiraling bands with red and white paint (rinsing brush well between colors), and paint the remaining areas blue. Paint the stars with matte paint. Allow to dry completely.

5 Place a few gold accent dots on the white stripes.

6 Fix the paint by baking as directed in the manufacturer's instructions.

AMERICA IS WOVEN OF MANY STRANDS; I WOULD RECOGNIZE THEM AND LET IT SO REMAIN...
OUR FATE IS TO BECOME ONE, AND YET MANY.
RALPH ELLISON

SILK DOOR SWAG

Preformed vine bases are available in a variety of shapes, including the arch-shaped base in this swag. Smaller versions can easily be created for indoor decorating if desired.

WHAT YOU NEED
Large vine swag base
Pipe cleaner
Glue gun
Assortment of silk and dried
    flowers in ivory and blue
Wire ribbon
Floral wire and cutters

1 Create a hanger with the pipe cleaner on the center back of the vine base.

2 Arrange your largest blooms down the sides of the arch, starting in the center and working outward with the stems facing the middle. Secure the blooms in place by adding a dab of hot glue at the bottom of each stem and inserting the stems into the vines.

3 Create a three-looped bow in the middle of your wire ribbon and secure it in place on the vine base with floral wire. Make a second bow to the left of the first bow, leaving about a foot of ribbon in between, then repeat on the right side. Attach the second and third bows as you did the first, then arrange the connecting ribbon as desired. Trim the ribbon ends, allowing about 3 inches of ribbon to drape off the base.

4 Fill in the remaining accent blooms around the ribbon, placing them with their stems facing the center.

COMPASSION IS NOT WEAKNESS, AND CONCERN FOR THE UNFORTUNATE IS NOT SOCIALISM.
HUBERT HUMPHREY

DESIGNER: CYNTHIA GILLOOLY

DESIGNER: MEGAN KIRBY

PATRIOTIC GEL CANDLES

Easy-to-make candles glow with patriotic pride to celebrate Fourth of July, Election Day, or "Welcome Home from Boot Camp!" When lit, they flicker in red, white, and blue.

WHAT YOU NEED
Clip-on pan thermometer
Pan
2 clear glass drinking glasses
Candle gel
Wick
Red and blue gel dyes
2 gold stars, approximately 2 inches tall
Metal skewer

1 Melt a small amount of gel in a pan over low heat to the highest temperature recommended by the manufacturer. Tint the gel blue, adding the pigment in small quantities until you've achieved the perfect color. (Tip: To find out exactly how your blue gel will look, place a tablespoon of the tinted gel on a piece of heavy white paper.) Pour the blue gel into the bottom third of each glass. Allow the gel to solidify completely (approximately 2 hours).

2 Clean your melting pan, taking care to remove all traces of the blue gel. Melt another small batch of gel and pour it into the middle third of the glasses. Allow the gel to sit for 2 minutes, then place a star in each glass and guide it into an upright position with the metal skewer. Allow the gel to solidify completely.

3 Repeat Step 1 for the top third of the glasses, this time tinting the gel red.

THE GREATEST HONOR HISTORY CAN BESTOW IS THE TITLE OF PEACEMAKER. THIS HONOR NOW BECKONS AMERICA... THIS IS OUR SUMMONS TO GREATNESS.

RICHARD NIXON

FOLK ART BANNER

Display your true colors by flying this red, white, and blue banner year-round. The rich color palette — denim blue, cranberry red, antique white, and butterscotch gold — enhances the custom appeal of the banner.

WHAT YOU NEED

2⅓ yards blue felt
1⅔ yards red felt
2 yards antique white felt
¼ yard gold felt
5 yards roll light, iron-on adhesive (or fusible web)
28-inch wooden dowel
#22 sharp chenille needle
3 skeins #5 black pearl cotton thread
7 assorted buttons
4 red buttons, 1 inch wide
Black puff paint, optional
Fabric glue, optional

1 Cut out two 24- x 54-inch rectangles, one from the blue felt and one from the red.

2 Cut out a 20- x 24-inch piece of blue felt. Match the sides and top of this piece with those of the red piece, and fuse them together with iron-on adhesive, covering all but a 1-inch border around the edge.

3 Photocopy the patterns on page 122 as directed. Create serpentine stripes with the white felt by repeating and joining outlines of pattern A in lengths. (The smallest stripes that fill the corners of the banner each measure approximately 11 inches long, the center stripe measures approximately 36 inches long, and the remaining two stripes measure approximately 26 inches long.) Cut each stripe several inches longer than you need it to allow for fitting it onto the banner.

4 Pin the longest stripe diagonally down the center of the banner, starting at the upper right corner and working to the lower left corner. Continue outward with the placement of the other four stripes, spacing them evenly. Iron the stripes in place, then trim the edges to fit the sides of the banner.

5 Use the chenille needle and black cotton thread to trim the sides of the stripes with a ½-inch blanket stitch. Blanket-stitch along the bottom of the blue square. (Alternatively, create faux stitches with black fabric paint.)

6 Iron a piece of adhesive to the back of the gold felt and cut out a large star from pattern B and six small stars from pattern C. Position the stars on the banner as pictured in the finished piece, and iron them in place. With black thread, create long accent stitches radiating from the stars onto the background. Sew a button in the center of each star. (Alternatively, create faux stitches with black fabric paint.)

7 Pin the striped banner face-up to the remaining piece of blue felt. Blanket-stitch around the edges of the two pieces to create the finished banner. (Alternatively, secure the two pieces together with fabric glue.)

8 Cut four 2- x 5-inch blue strips of felt for the vertical straps.

Fold one in half and overlap it on both sides of the banner about 2 inches in from the left side. Place the strip about 1½ inches down on the front and back of the piece. Evenly space and pin the other three strips in place along the top in the same position as the first. Stitch each in place by centering and sewing on a red button. Slide the dowel into the banner straps and display.

A PEOPLE WITHOUT HISTORY IS LIKE THE WIND ON THE BUFFALO GRASS.

SIOUX SAYING

DESIGNER: DEBI SCHMITZ

STATUE OF LIBERTY BANNER

Papel picado, the traditional Mexican folk art of cut paper, is a simple
way to create stunning banners. Although you can make the sections
of this banner in just about any size, keep in mind that the larger the
size, the easier it is to cut out the small details.

DESIGNER: KATHLEEN TRENCHARD

1 Enlarge the pattern on page 123 to the desired size. (17 x 12 inches is the traditional size.)

2 Cut three sheets, one each, of red, white, and blue tissue paper, about four inches larger on top than your enlarged pattern. Stack the tissues on top of the same size bond paper and place the pattern on top of the stack. The bond papers on top and bottom will protect the tissues and make cutting with a knife or scissors easier.

3 The bottom and sides should be flush with the edges of the pattern. The top should be left alone until cutting is complete and you are ready to attach the extra tissue on top to string.

4 Attach the tissues, bond paper, and pattern together with paper clips, pins, or staples in the gray areas outside the border.

5 Cut out only the gray shapes, starting with the tiny details in the center and working out toward the borders. Make use of the dotted fold lines in many of the shapes to be cut. These are symmetrical shapes that can be folded on the dotted lines and cut on the fold. Gray areas can be cut out by folding at the widest area, making a tiny snip on the fold, unfold, and insert the scissors to cut the whole shape out. This process will avoid punching the paper and potentially tearing it. No poking through the paper in needed. The nostrils of the statue are the only details that should be gently poked with a needle.

6 Continue holding the sheets together with paper clips on the outer edges until all of the gray is gone from your pattern. The border should be cut last, but not the top.

7 When cutting is complete, iron the sheets flat using a solid tissue on top to protect your cuttings.

8 To attach the string, lay the cut tissues in a row, leaving an inch or two between them. Apply a line of glue about an inch from the top of the sheets. Measure enough string so that you have a couple of feet of extra string on each side of your banners (for hanging). Stretch the string over the glue and fold each tissue over the string. Use string to hang the banner.

I AM THE
AMERICAN
HEARTBREAK,
THE ROCK UPON
WHICH FREEDOM
STUMPED ITS TOE.
LANGSTON HUGHES

NOTE: 10 sheets of tissue paper can be cut with a craft knife, 3 with sharp scissors.

TEMPLATES

DECOUPAGED BOOKMARK, PAGE 27; PHOTOCOPY AT 100%.

ETCHED OIL LAMPS, PAGE 30; PHOTOCOPY AT 100%.

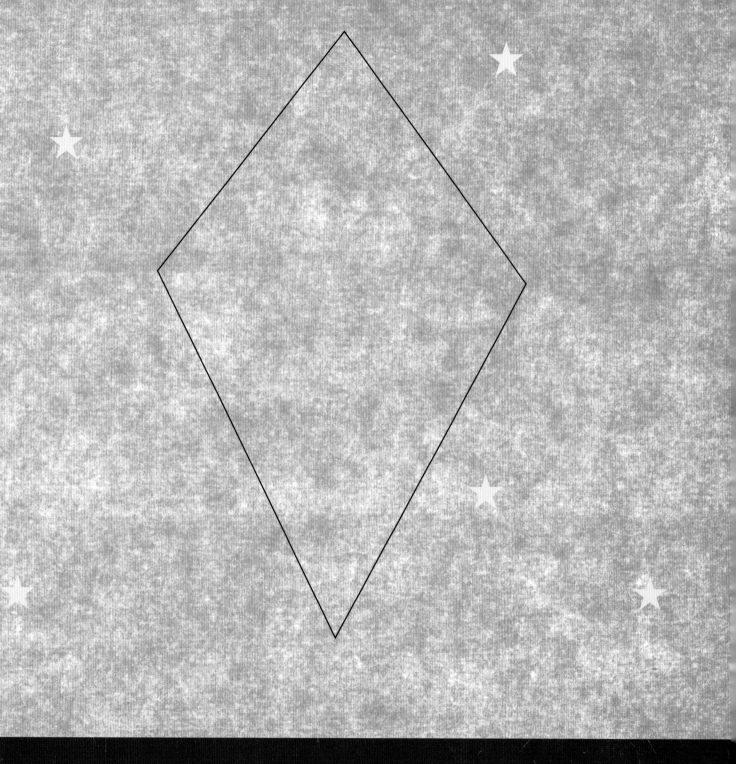

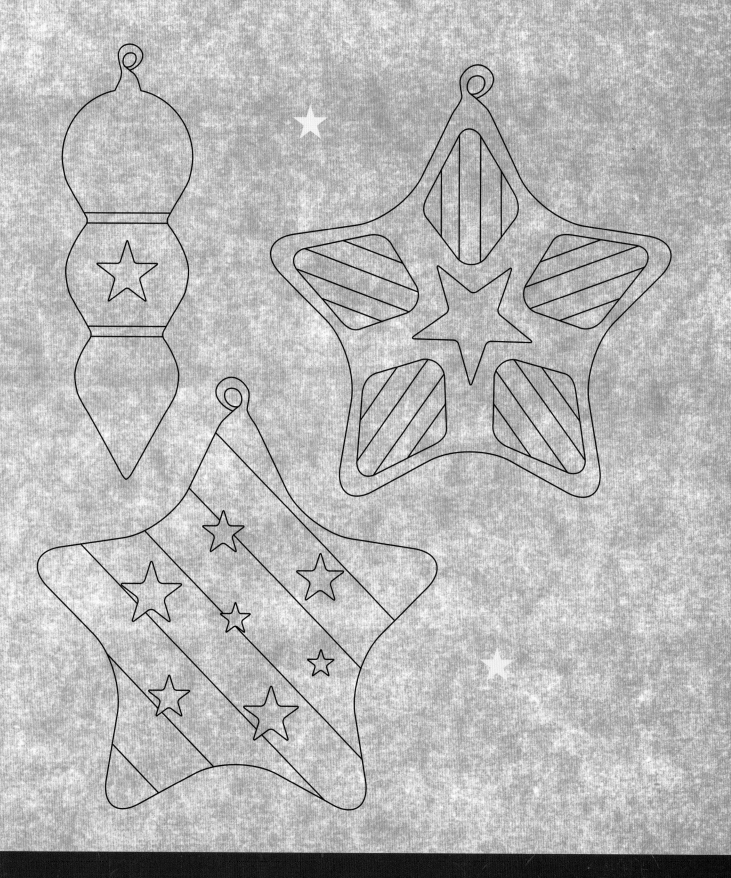

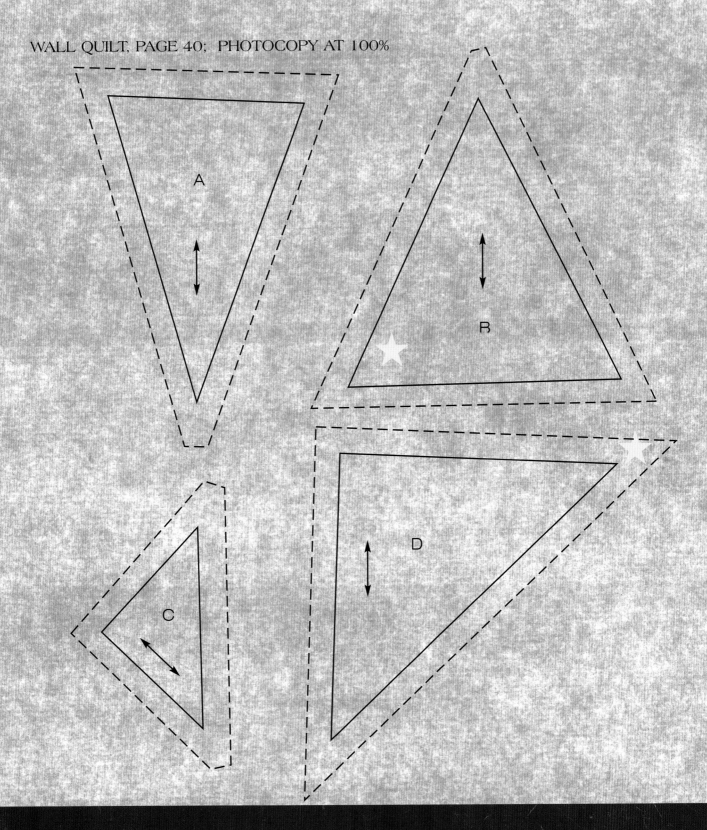

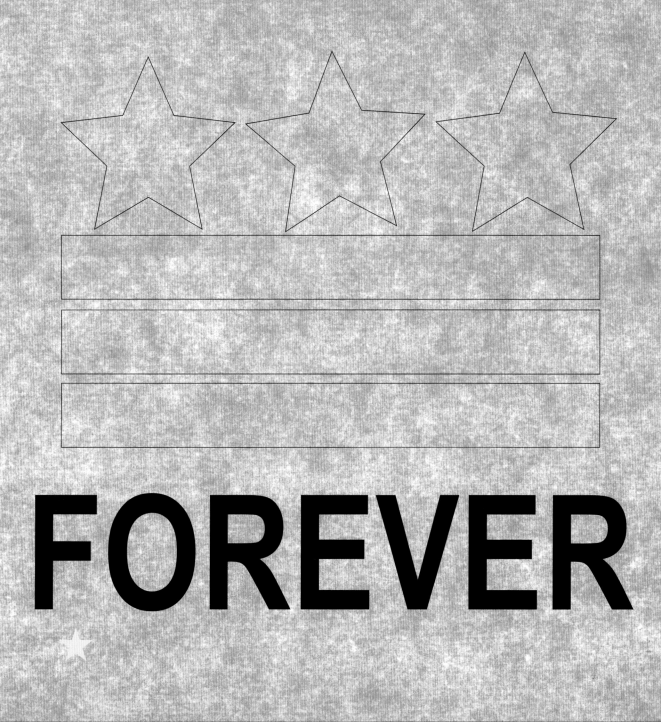

FOREVER

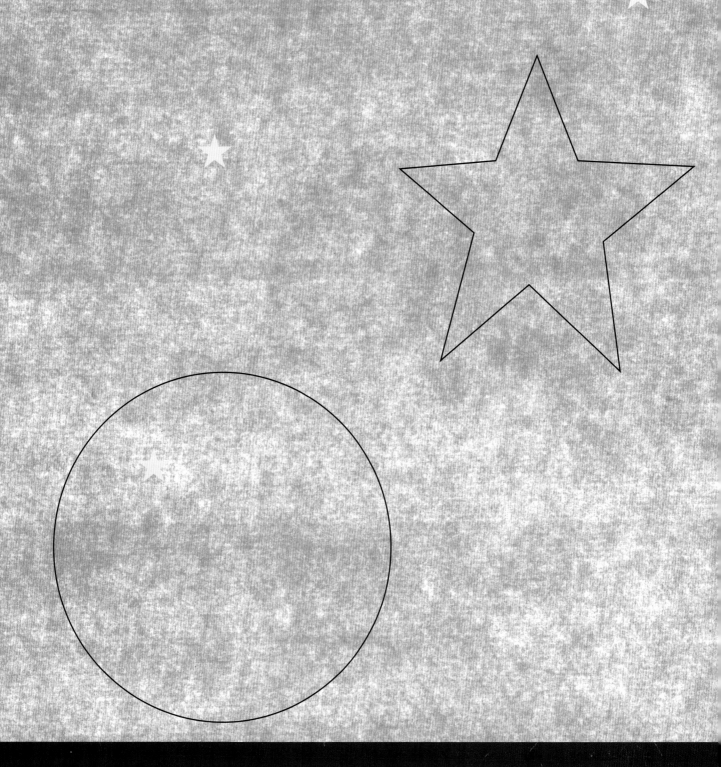

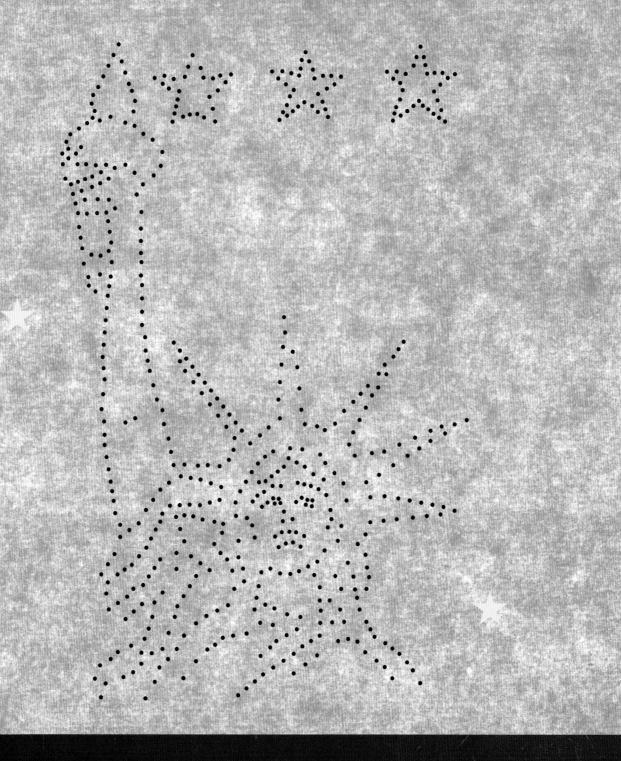

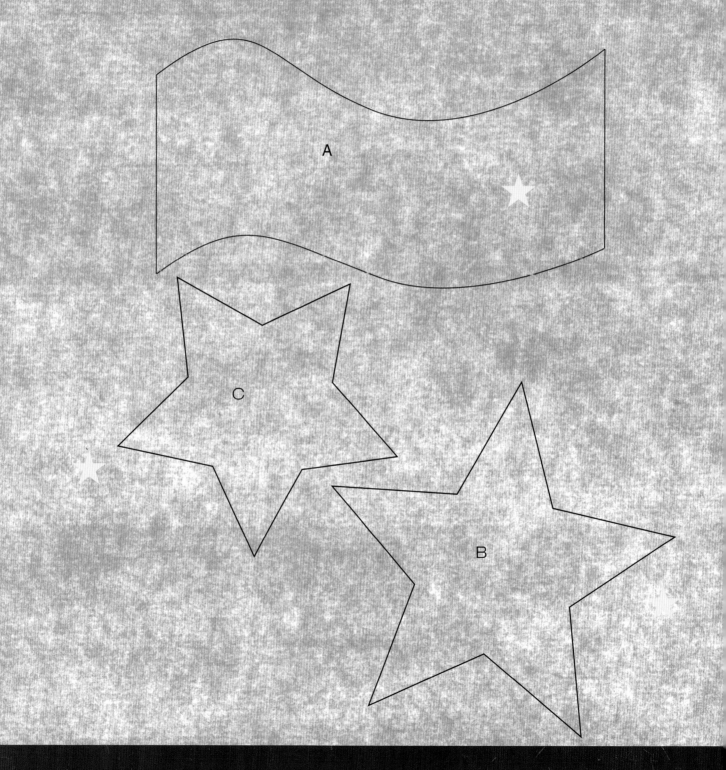

CONTRIBUTING DESIGNERS

KATHERINE AIMONE is an editor for Lark Books in Asheville, North Carolina. She has written books about stamping, collage, beading, and other subjects. In her spare time, she loves to join her husband, Steve, in their art studio to paint and play.

PENNY COTT maintains a private practice as a licensed professional counselor in Asheville, North Carolina. Raised in a home where her English grandmother exposed her to the bane of idle hands and the joy of home crafts, she was taught to knit and crochet as a child. She describes her creative projects as her "personal therapy."

CATHERINE HAM divides her time between homes in Austria, Greece, and the United States. She is never without her knitting bag when traveling, and finds it starts conversations in the most unusual places. Catherine is the author of *25 Gorgeous Sweaters for the Brand-New Knitter* (Lark Books).

TRACY HILDEBRAND is a glass beadmaker and jewelry artist. She makes her home in Asheville, NC, and is represented by galleries throughout the southeast.

DANA IRWIN has been an art director at Lark Books for 15 years. She spends her free time as an artist and freelance illustrator and a vegetable gardener of sorts. She also dabbles in puppet-making, and has a family of three dogs and two cats.

MEGAN KIRBY is an art director for Lark Books and *Fibcrarts* magazine. She makes her home in Asheville, North Carolina.

MARTHE LE VAN. Some kids mow the grass or do the dishes to earn their allowance. Not Marthe Le Van. Her painter-mom introduced her to the joys of framing at an early age. She garnered pocket money assembling metal frames and attaching hanging wires. This innocent task proved pivotal in Marthe's professional pursuits as a curator, exhibition manager, and craft designer. Marthe has created projects for several Lark publications, including *The Decorated Frame, Simple Glass Crafts, and Creative Tabletop Fountains.*

DIANA LIGHT lives and works in the Blue Ridge Mountains of North Carolina. After earning her BFA in painting and printmaking, she extended her expertise to etching and painting fine glass objects. She has contributed to numerous Lark Books and is the coauthor of Lark's *The Weekend Crafter: Etching Glass*.

BARBARA MATTHIESON lives in Washington State with her husband and, as she puts it, several extremely spoiled dogs and cats. Working with felt and combining it with other media is one of her favorite creative outlets.

JUANITA METCALF is certified by the National Quilter's Association as a teacher and a judge. She teaches workshops and gives lectures on a variety of quilting topics. Juanita operates a quilt shop, Juan's Quilt Cabin, in Clyde, North Carolina, and creates specialty items on consignment. She produces of a yearly art show at the Balsam Mountain Inn in Balsam, North Carolina, and her work has appeared in numerous Lark Books.

JILL MACKAY is an artist and designer who works out of her home in Pittsburgh, Pennsylvania. She is the author of *Creative Garden Mosaics, Dazzling Projects & Innovative Techniques* (Lark Books). She can be contacted at jmackay@lm.com.

JOAN K. MORRIS' artistic endeavors have led her down many successful creative paths. A childhood interest in sewing turned into professional costuming for motion pictures. After studying ceramics, Joan ran her own clay windchime business for 15 years. Since 1993, Joan's Asheville, North Carolina, coffee house, Vincent's Ear, has provided a vital meeting place for all varieties of artists and thinkers.

CHRIS RANKIN is a master crafter of all trades, having authored several books on dried flower crafts, a book on filet crochet, and, most recently, *Gel Candles* from Lark Books.

SALLY POOLE lives in Clemson, SC, where she is involved in many forms of needlework and crafts. An accomplished quilter, Sally has won awards for her work, and is known for her whimsical applique designs. She visits her native South Africa frequently, always returning with fresh inspiration for her projects.

DEBI SCHMITZ has been designing from her home in LeMars, Iowa, for more than ten years. She specializes in designs for felt and fabric as well as dolls. Her designs are quick and easy, to fit her busy life with her husband and four children.

TERRY TAYLOR lends his creative spirit full time to Lark Books, and, in his spare time, glues, pastes, and otherwise assembles works of art using a wide range of media from old CDs to broken china. His current interests include metal jewelry, and his work has been exhibed in many galleries and in many publications.

KATHLEEN TRENCHARD received her MFA in painting and printmaking from Pratt Institute. She discovered Mexican paper cutting when she moved to San Antonio, and authored the book *Mexican Papercutting* (Lark Books). Kathleen continues to collect and catalogue paper cuts during her travels throughout the globe. She can be contacted through her website: www.cut-it-out.org.

I KNOW THAT EVERY GOOD AND EXCELLENT THING IN THE WORLD STANDS MOMENT BY MOMENT ON THE RAZOR-EDGE OF DANGER AND MUST BE FOUGHT FOR…

THORNTON WILDER

INDEX

THE ONLY SURE BULWARK OF CONTINUING LIBERTY IS A GOVERNMENT STRONG ENOUGH TO PROTECT THE INTERESTS OF THE PEOPLE, AND A PEOPLE STRONG ENOUGH AND WELL ENOUGH INFORMED TO MAINTAIN ITS SOVEREIGN CONTROL OVER ITS GOVERNMENT.

FRANKLIN D. ROOSEVELT

A special thank you to Plymouth Yarn Company, Inc., for providing yarns for the projects on pages 48 and 62 through 66.

W E HOLD THESE TRUTHS TO BE SELF-EVIDENT,
THAT ALL MEN ARE CREATED EQUAL, THAT
THEY ARE ENDOWED BY THEIR CREATOR WITH
CERTAIN UNALIENABLE RIGHTS, THAT AMONG THESE
ARE LIFE, LIBERTY AND THE PURSUIT OF HAPPINESS.
THE DECLARATION OF INDEPENDENCE